THE
GLOBAL
GRADUATES

Amazing people on inspiring
extraordinary journeys

THE
GLOBAL
GRADUATES

Amazing people on inspiring extraordinary journeys

EDEM ADZAHO

Contents

Dedications

To God, for all I am and hope to be.
To my parents, for the sacrifices they made and the global doors they opened for me.
To my uncle, Honourable Edward Doe Adjaho for setting the pace and showing the importance of global collaborations.
To all the 35 Global Graduates featured in this book, this is your book. I put it together to celebrate you and inspire others.
You work hard and live remarkable lives and I have no doubt your stories are guaranteed to inspire all who will have a glimpse of your journeys.
Your journey so far is already changing lives: don't let anyone tell you any different!
This book is also dedicated to anyone (parents, guardians, mentors, bosses, friends…) who ever believed in you, encouraged, mentored and positively influenced you along the way.
I hope they will be proud to know they had a part to play in the person you have become or the person you are in the process of becoming.
To all the graduates across the globe, who are daring to be different.

Why I wrote this book

THE short, yet bold reason is to inspire and shape destinies!

The longer version… well, in 2004, I had returned to Ghana from the United Kingdom, after studying for a Master's degree. Although I had grown up in Ghana and had my primary, secondary and undergraduate education in Ghana, I came back home to no friends. All my friends were either in the USA, Canada or the UK. It was a challenging time indeed.

I had spent about 2 years in the UK and my time on the postgraduate course, plus living in the UK was one of the best years of my life: I met people from all over the world. And although it wasn't my first time experiencing the UK (I had spent several periods in London visiting my parents and taking short courses), my time studying for a full-time postgraduate degree was a totally different experience. I was on the right track to 'becoming', and it was exciting indeed.

But, in spite of all these exciting experiences and prospects, I had always said I did not want to be a 'statistic' after my studies, by staying on in the UK. I was coming back home to explore the possibilities: The most crucial one being a business idea I had whilst I was on my undergraduate programme. That idea is now an award winning human capacity development company, SPEC Consult Limited (www.spec-consult.com) a company I started in 2007.

SPEC Consult Limited has since 2012 also started the only Global Graduate Academy to train, coach and mentor the next generation of young African graduates to be Global Superstars who will represent the continent positively in business, entrepreneurship and leadership by thinking, acting and looking sharp.

I recall I did not struggle to find a job when I came back to Ghana. I was blessed enough to be thrown back into a multicultural environment and given the opportunity to work on global brands in one of the biggest advertising agencies in Accra. I made new friends, some of whom I have profiled in this book. Although it was competitive to get into the company, I probably took a lot for granted at the time. Looking back, I now know: I was different and had prepared for opportunities.

Not everyone easily got a job in a very dynamic company with a variety of global clients, and got assigned the huge responsibility of working on the biggest client in-house.

I was only able to put this into perspective when I started SPEC Consult and saw others struggle to sell themselves and find jobs. I saw what they were not doing and what they did wrong. I noticed a lot of graduates in my country were not confident: they had limited exposure, and more importantly, they were not prepared for opportunities, whether local or global. The shocking part is that most of these graduates and students were quick to say, "The world is a global village." I wondered if these self-proclaimed citizens of this global village knew what the culture, norms, behaviours and expectations of the decision makers of this "global village" were, particularly when they were hiring. I observed that most of these students and graduates saw the global village as a nice concept worth mentioning, but in practice, they were very clueless on how they could have a global mind-set to access opportunities, particularly in relation to jobs at home or anywhere else.

Three key things woke me up to finally crystallize the idea of speaking to and documenting the journeys of a few "citizens", particularly graduates who have earned their place.

I categorise these three key things as: the situations, the conversations and the people.

The Situations

Sometime in 2012, a series of events happened. The first, being that my Greek friend - with whom I studied on my Master's in England - contacted me in August of that year about coming to Ghana. He wanted to know if I knew about a company he was being headhunted for. He was living in London at the time and had just finished working on the London 2012 Olympics.

I was happy for my friend, and was also excited that we would be reconnected after ten years. As someone who is involved in graduate development, I thought, couldn't they find anyone as good as my friend in Ghana? It made me revisit the situation of the quality of talent available in my country. And I knew the reality: because, sadly, young graduates have not taken the time to ask who they want to be or how they can add value to themselves and be rounded and prepared for opportunities.

In the end, my friend took the offer as a restaurant manager for one of the most expensive restaurants in my city Accra. I knew most of the graduates in my country lacked exposure greatly and I wouldn't have been surprised if they became a fish out of water if they got the same opportunity as my Greek friend.

My friend has since moved to Kuwait, but not after making a stopover in Greece and Saudi Arabia for other job opportunities.

The second event was the realisation that having access to global opportunities wasn't necessarily about moving away from home. I myself had to work for 3 major brands present in over 100 countries without stepping out of Ghana. I also noticed high profile investors and companies were coming to Ghana, and I knew of some of the challenges companies like Goldman Sachs had faced in the past when they tried to find interns from Ghana. I had also been contacted by IBM via LinkedIn to recommend graduates for their Graduate Trainee Programme for their Ghana office. I couldn't find "the super stars", and I knew something had to change.

The Conversation

Sometime after 1:00 am on the 3rd of November 2012, I had a conversation with a friend on Skype. Our discussions finally gave me the inspiration to start thinking seriously about this book. And this is how the conversation went…

Vincent: Hello Boss how are you? Still up?

Edem Adzaho: Hey, trail blazer! Yep, where are you?

Vincent: In Paris, by God's grace.

Edem Adzaho: Cool. Well done. I am so proud of you. So your French is perfect now, I guess.

Vincent: one of my goals for opting for Paris was to learn the language.

Vincent: I often go to a hang-out called franglish, where French people interested in learning English meet up with English speakers keen on learning French.

Vincent: I arrived in February this year, but returned to Scotland for a month, then came back in mid-March, stayed until July, and left after six weeks on another assignment in Scotland. Then I came back in September and left for the US for another month, so it's been quite on and off.

Vincent: What is your current project? The breadth of people you've trained is overwhelming... Great things truly have humble beginnings and God does marvellous things in His time. Wow!

Edem Adzaho: I know and I am grateful.

Edem Adzaho: We are looking for people with leadership potential, I know it sounds like a cliché, but it's true. A track record in their proven area of proposed study; good communicators; people who can think and will be ambassadors for Ghana. I stopped doing the graduate thing for a while.

Vincent: I guess it got annoying dealing with young guys who got no clue about what they want to achieve in life, or more specifically, have not invested much in developing themselves... Instead of finding it tough to select people because of extreme and great competence, it ended up being the other way round

Edem Adzaho: So what have you been up too?

Vincent: I've done Financial planning and analysis for our Oil & Gas business in Aberdeen and Angola, built financial systems in Qatar for our Gas turbine service business there, after Treasury operations in Australia and New Zealand. I came home for a month, and then they recalled me to their Middle East Airlines headquarters in Dubai. I set up financial rhythms for their joint venture with Abu Dhabi. I did internal audit across 22 countries within Middle East and Africa…Now I am on an acquisition integration project for an Energy business we bought here. I then moved to Paris in Feb to help with risk management for our aviation arm.

Edem Adzaho: Wow! I am writing a book: you are probably one of the best people to help out.

Vincent: Sure, no problem. More importantly, I am trying to see how I can leverage all these experiences when I return home and as soon as I am led by God to return.

Vincent: I caught up with Dalia and Saulius... and they really spoke highly of you. Your drive to excel, plus you have a different mindset from the typical Ghanaians they encountered.

Edem Adzaho: He takes us from humble backgrounds and changes our stories.

Vincent: Yes, he does. Let's catch up again soon. Ciao.
Edem Adzaho: Salut.

The People

After the above conversation, I knew there was hope, because I have at first hand interacted with people like Vincent, right here in Ghana and across the globe. These are everyday people who push the envelope to do extraordinary things. Most of the people I profiled in this book have a connection with Africa: Non Africans who have sought opportunities on the continent and excelled, and the Africans who are making a mark on the continent or act as good ambassadors for the African continent. It is only natural, that as a Ghanaian, the majority of the people I profiled are people I know and met in Ghana.

I wrote this book to celebrate these people and to show others the way. For one reason, or another, I couldn't interview other equally amazing people whose careers I have watched closely, people like:

- David Afflu, a global graduate in every shape and form. David worked for Nestlé Ghana, Shell, Vodafone and is now with PZ Cussons as the Commercial Director.
- Kuorkor Dzani is currently an Executive Director for NDK Financial Services. She has worked at Stanbic Bank Ghana, The Central Bank of Ghana and Standard Bank Advisory in China.
- Elizabeth Biney-Amissah, a Princeton alumni with a major in Molecular Biology and a Chinese Language and Culture Certificate who has since exchanged Wall Street for Accra.

- Nana Kofi Acquah, who previously worked on various international brands as a Creative Director and a Copy Writer. Nana is now an international photographer, capturing the lives of everyday hardworking rural folks in Burkina Faso, Cote d'Ivoire, Mali and Ghana, for International Clients like Nestlé. His footprints are in Mauritius, Democratic Republic of Congo and many other corporate clients. He is also a sought-after photographer for celebrities and high profile executives. Nana's work can equally be found in boardrooms across the globe and has been featured on global news channels like CNN and BBC.
- Naa Amerley Croffie, who at one time was managing operations and contracts in her capacity as a Human Resources and Legal Executive on her company's behalf in Ghana, Uganda and Denmark.
- Anneline Johns, whose career has taken her from Zimbabwe, to research in Warsaw, and she is now in charge of a chain of high-end pubs in London.
- Emmanuel Sackey, whom I coached briefly, but he also added value to himself and right here in Ghana has been in various business development roles at a global HR franchise, a Japanese company, and now he is with the Danish Embassy in Ghana.
- Morris Ofori – Mensah whose career with Tigo, (Millicom Ghana) has taken him to Tanzania, Congo and London. Morris is now in the USA to study and map out the next chapter.

I know there are many more people out there. People who we have all crossed paths with at some point, but have never really bothered to find out who they really are and why they are on a certain track.

Their CVs or resumes don't always capture the entire story. Hopefully this book does.

PS: A little side note about grammar- Although I know and love it, I haven't always followed it in this book. Sometimes I start sentences with and, but and because… I use plural they, their in contexts that sometimes require the singular he or she. I also use didn't, it's couldn't and a few others. I did this for immediacy and informality, and hopefully the sticklers will understand and forgive me.

As I shared the stories, I didn't see the need to change what they have said from American English to British English or vice versa. They are global graduates after all.

Let's go meet them.

Petra Lieb

WITH all the negative news we are bombarded with in the media, one cannot help but admire a young dynamic lady who moves to Pakistan for work.

Petra is one of the inspirations for this book. I met her about 6 years ago in Ghana, and I could instinctively feel her drive and positive energy. It helped that her opinions were always refreshing too.

Petra never thought she would leave her home country of Romania. Growing up in a communist country, her generation was the first to graduate after communism and she was such an advocate when it came to promoting her region.

After University, she went for a series of interviews for limited job opportunities, which were so competitive. In the end, she started working in sales departments of various car dealerships.

She changed to work with Horus Development and Finance as a potential path of entry to the banking system- as initially mapped out in her career plan.

Petra was also interested in a loan officer opportunity as a way to learn the trade. About 9 months into the job, she moved into Consulting, and things changed quickly from there.

The one person who influenced her to start thinking in a global direction was her boss at the time, Mr. Degoy. Just when her two-year project ended, her boss asked her if she wanted to go to Ghana. This offer though was conditional: her life would be synonymous with travel. In a nutshell, the travelling would never stop.

She took the advice of her boss to pursue her first direct international assignment in Ghana. The supposed three-month contract in Ghana turned to three years. Petra has since moved on and made her mark in Cameroon, Tanzania and Nigeria, and she currently works in Pakistan.

Her company is a Francophone micro finance consulting company with global networks. When her company was looking to start projects in Anglophone countries, she became the first candidate to be considered because of her language skills. Knowing English as a second language was a real asset, as everyone else wanted to go to the francophone countries within the global network for the same limited opportunities.

Working for the same consulting company in Pakistan, her current role as a Consultant, is focusing on micro finance setups, and she is responsible for training, IT, and the operations team of the bank.

In Pakistan, Petra had no team to start off with, but she has been able to select, train and grow the team to be good professionals in the banking sector, as well as valuable members of their teams.

Although a huge part of her job is setting up banking operations from the scratch, the social impact of her job excites her more. Petra is actively involved in training her young Pakistani staff on a variety of high-level skills. Her job, in essence, is about training minds: moulding young minds to appreciate professionalism, so they can function not just within her organisation, but will be capable wherever they go.

Petra has a wealth of knowledge and insight from all the countries she has worked in. For instance, living in a culture that is completely different from her European roots, she has to deal with the dynamics of culture as a young woman in Pakistan, from the way she conducts herself as a woman, to her choice of clothes, in both professional and social circles.

As a keen observer of every step of operations and implementation, she realises that in Pakistan, the existing methodology and training materials do not always work, even though it has been successful everywhere else. This means she had to adopt a different approach, which is more tailored towards local needs.

In Tanzania, her challenge was getting staff to understand aspects of professionalism on a consistent basis.

In Nigeria, she was shocked in a good way, by the energy the staff would put into what they believed in. Even though she noticed a common trait of young Nigerians wanting to have their way, she also observed that once you articulate your vision clearly and outline what is to be achieved, you will have their 100% committed input. She was also impressed by how young Nigerians liked to use their minds, are fearless and will always come out of 3 of every 5 challenging situations.

Petra found Nigeria inspiring. She says, "You teach them one thing, and they want to turn it around. They thrive on a challenge." In Ghana, she observed that the speed, understanding and logic with which people approached things was different. She realised it was important to not only teach staff the important things, but to also learn from them. That way, the team feels you are on the same page with them and only then will they strive to do better.

Petra's global outlook is driven by the fact that each country will develop at its own pace, and knowing that she has the skills to fit anywhere; she is at a great advantage for this global journey.

As her career progresses, Petra will like to develop her management skills more. Her broad vision in the long-term is to focus on all aspects of strategy, particularly when it comes to the micro-finance banking environment.

For Petra, to succeed globally means having a dream and being inspired to work for it. Petra is inspired by people who achieve things others could not achieve. Interestingly, I am inspired by Petra venturing into territories I am not bold enough to venture into yet.

Petra's challenge as a global graduate is how difficult it can be when she goes home. She points out that her timing is not the same as that of her peers and, "The conversations are different too: it's not always easy to explain the cultural differences, the taste of the food in one country or another."

Also, packing to go back home can be a real challenge. For a start, nothing ever fits into her luggage. Her luggage is never big enough to carry the 'world' with her, and she always has to leave things behind.

Another challenge is making the effort to have appropriate local outfits, and the constant need to edit and review her wardrobe; something every professional woman across the globe can somewhat relate to. She is not complaining, as the thrill and adventure of constant travel beats the odds.

Her advice to graduates the world over is, "You don't have to be afraid. Dream of what you want, and be free to explore it."

Petra generally sees young Africans as nice people who have tremendous potential, and because she has interacted with young Africans from both East and West Africa, on various levels, she has some food for thought for them. She sees so much potential on the continent. Her simple advice to young Africans is to 'step out of their comfort zones, because if Africa will change, it is only the young Africans who can effect that change'.

Lucien Hoogenbosch

With Lucien in the Netherlands

LUCIEN was the first person I interviewed, and I was lucky enough to meet him in The Netherlands. This was just before he caught his flight to St. Petersburg in Russia with a group, as part of his summer holidays. I was also due to catch a train to Antwerp after my interview with him, and then connect to Zurich.

As he told me about his upcoming trip, I was just as excited to tell him about the many countries I was about to visit to interview people like him.

Everywhere we turned, there were global brands to

remind us of the topic to be discussed: What it means to be a global graduate. Luck was on our side, as we did not have to look very far for inspiration to kick the interview off. We sat under a Heineken branded umbrella and drank Lipton ice tea, while I got my set of Energizer batteries ready for my recorder to record the interview.

Lucien wanted to be a skiing instructor as he has been skiing since the age of 4 and loves it. Interestingly, he has had stints as a skiing instructor, teaching others to ski, and he thinks kids make the best students, because they are flexible, and have no fear.

One of Lucien's past jobs was working at the post office as a deliveryman. Even with this job, he learnt a lot of transferable skills that he uses in his current job as a high school Geography Teacher. Very useful everyday skills such as communication and learning to deal with different kinds of people from different backgrounds were some of them. Learning to manoeuvre his van through narrow streets, in addition to getting the experience of planning ahead as there were multiple routes to cover, led him to gain further skills in planning, as well as saving cost for his employers.

At University, Lucien knew he was good at Geography and Economics, but there were about 400 people opting to study Economics and he did not want to be like everybody else. He opted for Geography instead. His passion to be a teacher was quite obvious during his interview and it comes as no surprise to find Lucien currently teaching Geography to 12 to18 year olds in high school.

Noticing a gap to teach the subject in schools, coupled with his general love for geography and seeking knowledge, he undertook another Master's degree after the first one in Geography. Lucien's second Master's degree is in Teaching Skills and Class Management. Armed with two Master's degrees, he was ready for future opportunities.

Another reason why Lucien likes teaching Geography, is because it is about teaching the world: nature and people and how human interactions change the world in different ways. He suggests we look around us, because there is geography everywhere.

Getting into his current role was quite competitive. He points out how the government in The Netherlands is encouraging a lot of people to get into teaching, because there is a shortage of teachers. Hence, there are a number of very qualified people seeking the same opportunities. He realised having a higher degree (in his case another Master's degree), specific to teaching and class management did give him the edge, which of course opens doors to more opportunities and a better salary.

Ever the knowledge seeker, Lucien has pretty much seen almost the whole of Europe. Some of the countries he has been to are: Slovenia, Germany, France, Czech Republic, Denmark, Luxembourg, England and Greece. He has also been to Cuba, China, Ghana, and many others. He has not only worked in his native Holland, but has ventured out for opportunities in Ghana and Austria.

For someone who chose his first Master's degree strategically, to explore his interest in the environment and teaching, an opportunity for him to do research work with two PhD fellows in Ghana came up. He seized the opportunity to come to Ghana because he realised that as you grow older, you might not always have the opportunity to experience things with your whole family like he was used to. He also saw it as a way to learn something new in Ghana. He is glad to say, not only was it a useful experience for him, but his thesis was also used by the PhD fellows in other publications. This is something he is very happy about.

Lucien has found a way to bring the world to the classroom, as his many experiences have taught him that children like stories from across the globe. His travels have added value to his teaching skills. He points out "teaching just by the book is not right and clearly not for me."

Lucien thinks it is a useful experience for teachers to go on excursions and school trips. He has used actual personal photos taken during visits to Elmina Castle in Ghana, to teach his students back home in The Netherlands.

In the future, he is keen on exploring the opportunity for teachers in The Netherlands to take part in an exchange programme for teachers to teach in Ethiopia and Kenya.

Although a knowledge seeker, Lucien does not see himself researching all the time, and he is not considering a PhD anytime soon. One thing I can predict is that his desire to travel would not stop, and this is something his students will always be grateful for, because each travel will come with a unique story and educational photos.

The most useful skill he brings to the job is being able to see geography everywhere, because this enhances his knowledge in an interesting way, and he is able to share this with his students. Because of Lucien, I found myself collecting volcanic rocks, lava and moss in Iceland, so I can donate it to any geography department that might need it.

To Lucien, the love for teaching is not just about sharing knowledge, but seeing the progress of his students. And just as he can tell a feeling of pride on the faces of his own past teachers, he equally feels a sense of pride every time a student makes progress.

Lucien's own global encounter began when he went camping in France and Italy in a caravan with his parents, as a young boy. His first trip outside Europe was to Hong Kong as part of an exchange programme between Dutch and Chinese Students.

He is aware that communication problems is one of the challenges of a being a global graduate. For instance, not knowing the main language of your host country and not understanding other non-verbal communication cues can be a real challenge. Apart from Dutch, Lucien speaks fluent English, German, and a little French. He encourages all students, especially those from China and Asia to make an effort to learn other languages. For him, apart from travel, another good introduction to a global mindset is the various languages such as French, German, Italian and Spanish. He was taught these at school, and he made the effort to learn them. He believes these languages are still being taught in some schools, but if that is not the case, students should find ways to learn some of these languages.

His advice for future graduates is that they should "Explore, because the world is bigger than Facebook."

Lucien says, "A global graduate is someone who has the opportunity to work not only in your home country, but anywhere you like." He was quick to point out that one of the skills needed to be a global graduate, is to travel, as travel can be a useful way to meet local people, because local people have more local knowledge to share. He advises, "Don't just travel by being on the bus and taking photos." He even suggests it is important to "Explore your own country if you can." That's something I did in 2010, when I was backpacking through Northern Ghana, which led to me meeting Lucien and building the network for the future.

For him, if you want to be global, then think about being the best. He believes everybody is good at something, and it is important to know what you are good at. Also, choosing a career path early with some parental or professional help is also crucial, because it will help one identify what they are good at: whether it is science, cultural issues, languages, or even politics. Lucien strongly believes if you don't know what to do, then that can be very tough.

If he had to do it all over again, he will do the same thing, because with Geography, he can also specialise in issues to do with managing or planning the environment.

Lucien thinks it is good to have University level education, because at that level, you are trained to be introspective, analytical, form your own opinions and ideas, and take initiative. He suggests that even if you are not being trained to do so, you should find ways to do that yourself.

Adam Romanowski

ADAM'S global journey is one of purpose and intrigue.

If you put Adam in a certain box because he has a Master's in Marketing and Management from Warsaw School of Economics, and an additional specialisation in Project Management, a semester as an MBA exchange student at the Asian Institute of Management in Manila (Philippines), you will be holding the wrong box, because he won't fit in it. Adam is not that predictable!

Born in a small family in communist Poland, Adam confesses he did not always have a global mindset. Full of insight, Adam explains that being a closed communistic country for over 40 years, did not allow people to develop a global mindset, know and understand cultural differences or the importance of being exposed to foreigners. As a result, his "youth was mostly concentrated on the things that were within the country's frontiers", and only after some time, he started to realise that like the lyrics of Matt Costa's song, "But there's a big wide beautiful world out there. For those that want it, it's out there."

Though on a personal level, he knew his values, priorities and what he wanted to achieve, it was not quite the case when it came to what he wanted to do professionally. He however used his personal values and principles to help him choose the next steps for his professional life. Adam admits he got to where he is now by adopting a positive attitude, being open to opportunities, and not being afraid of change and challenges.

And with new ideas always coming to his mind, Adam always recognised that the possibilities with what he can do with his life are endless. He considered and still considers different career paths; from being a coast guard, or setting up his own social enterprise, to becoming a CEO for one of the global companies. He does, however, realise that with the passing of time, his choices are not becoming easier but different. Adam is in the meantime getting experience in various roles and checking whether they are what he would like to pursue for his future career. He sees this phase as an opportunity to be able to choose what is next and get closer to what he wants in life.

Not too long ago, Adam was in Zambia to work for an

NGO. He and his partner decided to quit their jobs and start a "journey". A journey through unknown lands, giving back to local people, and discovering what was next for them both. Although there were a lot of question marks along the way, one thing they knew for sure was the importance of taking that six-month journey together. They travelled beyond Zambia to pretty much all of Southern Africa. This comes as no surprise, as one of Adams's mantras is to "Remember to never stop searching for who you want to be; dream big; don't be afraid of making it happen; and share your happiness with others."

Adam's first global encounter was an eye-opening trip. He travelled alone to the USA to visit his family for the summer holidays. He was only 17 and it was the first time he sat on a big plane to leave the European continent behind. During his two-month stay, he discovered many interesting people out there in the world with different ideas, opinions and lifestyles. More importantly he realised how beautiful the world is and how it felt to be independent and free. On his way back home, he just knew he wanted more of "that" experience in his life. He figured out quite quickly that the only way to experience "more" was to come back home and work hard, day and night and get to the best University that will provide him with the endless opportunities for his future. A future he says, "Will help me follow my dreams and sit one more time on a big plane." Adam kept his dreams alive and worked towards them.

He started gaining work experience in high school, working at a conference centre and being a lifeguard. After that came University and his true love for travelling. The only challenge he had to overcome was lack of funds, to which he says, turned to be the best thing that could happen to him. Because when he started his studies he would use all his summer breaks to go abroad and work. The money he earned was sufficient to allow him to experience the local life and travel around. He started with printing more than 100 copies of his CV and a one-way ticket to Brighton (England). After hours of wandering from restaurant to restaurant and giving out his CVs he finally got the opportunity to become a waiter. The following year, he was on the other side of the world, lifeguarding in one of the aqua parks in the US. After coming back home, he decided to take on an opportunity in a field that was more related to his studies, and ended up doing his internship with EURO RSCG, one of the global advertising agencies. That same year, his will to travel, discover and learn grew even stronger, and this led him to Accra (Ghana). During his semester break, he worked as a Marketing Officer at Nissan and Volkswagen. The year after that, he went for his University exchange in the Philippines and put all his efforts towards graduating and receiving his diploma. After he had submitted his thesis and was waiting for the final exam, he started his job as a Brand Marketing Associate at Danone, giving him the chance to learn a lot about the FMCG sector. With less than a year in the company, he decided to change the location for a warmer place, and moved to Lisbon, Portugal, to take on a Marketing and Product Innovation Assistant role for Conceito O2, an HR consulting company, which happens to be one of the biggest HR consulting companies on the local market.

Adam's dream was to always live in a small house by

the ocean and be able to surf every day. And he found the opportunity to do so when he got on a 1-year graduate program for VMware in Singapore and Australia.

But, before this big move, misfortune struck and he says of that period, "It was one of the toughest periods in my life, because a couple of weeks before, tragedy struck. I lost the closest person in my life, my best friend, at the age of 24. He died in a car accident. And after spending a week in Poland, I knew that I needed to change something. The world is too big and beautiful to be sitting in one place. And you never know when your time will come, so you should use every day as if it was your last, look for happiness in small and simple things and share it with others. I started to look for various opportunities on websites with job offerings from all over the world as well as student websites with opportunities in exciting locations." This opportunity presented itself as VMware.

And even though he did not have any experience in IT and his knowledge in that field was limited to Microsoft Office tools and browsing the Internet, he knew this was it. He saw it as an opportunity that would allow him to grow and learn about a new and exciting industry in the fastest growing economies, as well as fulfil his dream of living in a small hut by the ocean.

Adam credits AIESEC, the international student organisation that allows young ambitious individuals to work all around the globe in their fields of interest, for part of his rise. AIESEC as an organisation, he says, provides many opportunities for its members. For Adam, AIESEC makes everything possible, but he mentions, "It was definitely competitive like most of the job offers nowadays." And with the right preparation, a positive attitude, and four interviews later, he was packing his bags to change his life completely, one more time.

For over two years he was in Singapore, developing professionally in VMware as a Partner Programs Manager in Asia Pacific and Japan (APJ). Adam worked hard, visited many countries, and was part of multiple projects on his graduate program.

The combination of work at one of the global IT leaders, together with one of the fastest growing economies of Asia gave him a lot of opportunities and challenges daily. Most importantly, it allowed him to constantly learn, work with people from different cultures and multiple countries as well as continue his passion of travelling and sports. Adams says he spent most of his free time with his backpack, camera and friends, getting to know new places and constantly discovering himself and looking for inspiration.

It was not all about travelling. Adam spent the time to be grateful for what he has in life and try to give back to others by leading and being involved in multiple volunteering projects across APJ.

And it wasn't all "work" either, because even Adam's "play" is not conventional.

One of Adam's photos was chosen as a favourite for Daily Dozen pictures in the iconic National Geographic magazine and was posted on the editor's spotlight blog.

He has participated in multiple international races; starting from Half Ironman Triathlon in Malaysia (1.9 km swim / 90 km bike ride / 21.1km run), Marathons in Poland

and the Great Wall of China, as well as many others, including a 100km team race in the mountains of Hong Kong to raise $10k funds for Oxfam – one of the global NGOs fighting against poverty in multiple countries around the world.

Adam thinks one of the big challenges of being in a global environment is the overload of data, devices and information thrown at us. He is of the view that the new generation of young people need to learn how to search and process information fast, as well as be efficient in the way they communicate with each other. He notes that the right data and time required to process it is crucial, but at the same time it is important not to lose ourselves in the Internet, phones, phone calls and the world of social media too much, at the cost of our personal relationships. He also advised that, we need to remember that all those devices will never replace the simple act of hugging somebody, or carrying on face-to-face conversation when needed.

Like all the people profiled in this book, I wanted to know if there was any one person, thing or situation that has influenced Adam's thinking in a global direction. Adam says it is difficult to find one person, thing or situation, but there were multiple moments that brought him to the place he is now, he notes. "I think my biggest influencers during my youth were my parents. Even though they were not travelling a lot, one of the things that they taught me - and it helped me to think in a global direction - was not to look at others when we want to do something, and even though we might be afraid to do things alone and in a different way, if we are confident, positive and believe in them, we should pursue them: it's our life. Who we are is up to us, and our decisions.

And it's only us who can decide which way to go. Our biggest privilege is to be free, and we shouldn't waste this."

Some of the lessons Adam has learnt along the way are:

"Always question the processes, projects and what you are doing… only by doing so will you be able to understand, improve and show your value."

"Understand the big picture: by knowing how your everyday work impacts the overall business, you will become more engaged and motivated."

"It's all about people: no matter how exciting, big or small the company you are working in is, the people you are working with will make you grow. Look for an environment that will stimulate you and help you develop. Look for a good mentor and a passionate team."

"Don't be afraid to challenge yourself and take risks: it's the most effective way to learn: there will be multiple times you will fail but those are the moments that will shape your success."

"Give back: A simple smile from the other person is the only thing that matters at the end of the day. Find a way to share your professional skills in order to help others, you will learn new things about yourself and answer questions you never thought of asking. Think positive: your attitude will help you to pave the way to success and make friends for the rest of your life."

Adam agrees, "Everybody is unique in this world, with great potential and strengths that could lead to success. There is not one perfect combination of skills or attitude, but the most important is remember to be yourself, enjoy what you are doing, and be passionate about it. If I would have to point the most important things that brought me to where I am now, it would be: having a positive attitude, confidence, motivation and empathy. All the rest can be learned."

One of the most important skills he needed to learn fast from the very beginning of his international career was the ability to adapt fast to local cultures. He says, "even though our world is getting smaller, thanks to globalisation, there are and will always be major differences in people's behaviour, attitude and thinking, based on the regional culture, corporate culture or individual backgrounds. In order to succeed professionally in the international world, we need to be able to get rid of all the assumptions, expectations and norms we are used to, as they are our worst enemies. We should spend some time observing and trying to understand how people think, act and communicate in different places, and only by doing so, we will be able to efficiently cooperate with them. At the same time, we shouldn't lose our identity and the positive attitude we have towards certain things, but rather be mindful and empathic towards others and their way of being."

To date, Adam has been to over 50 countries across all continents, lived and worked in 8 countries (Poland, England, US, Ghana, Portugal, Singapore, Australia and Zambia), and studied in 2. So being a global graduate for Adam, "…is all about open mindset, seeing possibilities not barriers, seeing solutions not roadblocks, having ideas and not being afraid to stand up for them and act. If I were hiring a recent graduate, I will look for an open mindset, a positive attitude, passion, empathy and willingness to learn."

Adam now works for a tech company in Silicon Valley

and has a lot of advice for graduates who want to succeed globally. He says, "You need to believe in yourself, follow your passions and not be afraid of getting out of your comfort zone. Be patient and search, act and prepare yourself to stand up after the failure. If you thank your failures and learn from them, you will be able to succeed in life."

Another thing that helped him tremendously was his language skills. He advises that, if you want to increase your chances in the global world, learn foreign languages: one or two, because the more languages one can speak, the better it is for the individual in terms of opportunities and mobility. Because, being able to speak foreign languages, Adam agrees, one is "able to multiply opportunities for their future careers", and "most importantly, learn new things, discover other cultures and understand more people." Adams also advises that, irrespective of where we come from, each and every single one of us has something unique to offer and give, both in our professional life as well as in our personal environment. Adam encourages young people to engage with various organisations like AIESEC, which is a great example of how young people can grow their skills through global internships, leadership roles and simply interacting with other ambitious fresh graduates.

He also stressed on the importance of always trying to develop one's self professionally and personally in the areas of one's interests, because that way, you will be able to maintain a healthy work-life balance. And in connection with that, Adam is keen on getting a skydiving certification.

When I asked Adam if he would do anything differently, his response is really inspiring. He says, "Most people would probably answer by saying, no, I am happy with who and where I am and wouldn't change anything, but my answer is yes, because, I would like to say thank you a couple more times, give a couple more hugs to people I love, and smile to a couple more strangers. Life is all about small things that make us and the world we live in a better place." Apart from that, we should believe, keep looking and smiling, because there is always a way to achieve the things we want and we should remember to make sure we are enjoying the journey, otherwise it will be a waste of time.

Misha Njeri Madsen

With Misha in Paris

MISHA is from Nairobi, Kenya and currently lives in Denmark, where she has just graduated with an MSc in International Marketing and Management from Copenhagen Business School.

I could not meet Misha in Denmark, but she was kind enough to meet me in Paris for her interview. After we had checked out the sites and shopped, we took a break for coffee in a café behind the Notre Dame Cathedral to talk about her journey as a global graduate.

Misha has visited Ethiopia, Mozambique, South Africa, Cote d'Ivoire, Togo, France, Spain, Norway, Italy, Switzerland, Hungary, Poland, UK, Ireland and many others.

At the last count, Misha has worked in Ghana, Kenya and Denmark and has attended several conferences in countries like Cameroon, Tanzania, Uganda and India.

Although she originally wanted to go to Egypt for an AIESEC job, she found herself in Ghana instead. Ghana then became the home of Misha's first real international job. In Ghana, she worked at the national office of AIESEC and was responsible for marketing AIESEC and managing AIESEC's corporate partnerships and coaching members on AIESEC's brand and philosophy. She also collaborated on various projects and programmes and facilitated alumnus networking events. Her time in AIESEC led to AIESEC's first ever-annual report in 20 years to be produced for Ghana. She then worked with the advertising giant MMRS Ogilvy in Ghana.

Before Ghana, she was a project officer for Gatsby Trust in Kenya, and after Ghana, she worked with Standard Charted Bank in Kenya as a Customer Service Support Officer.

Even in Kenya, Misha had a connection with Denmark, because whilst still working with Standard Chartered, she was keen to further her international experience, and MYC4, a Danish microfinance company with an online financing platform, was also looking to hire an African, preferably Kenyan, to fill the role of Partner Relations Coordinator.

Though it was a competitive role to get into, Misha was ready when opportunity struck and a contact was facilitated by AIESEC for a six-month internship.

Misha had a key role in establishing MYC4 in Kenya, together with a director and an office administrator. She was responsible for developing and managing relationships with the business partners and contributed to setting up systems to approach new partners. Misha was also very instrumental in developing the microfinance platform competency level of the business partners, as well as the training manual for the company, when a new platform was launched.

With MYC4 present in Ghana, Tanzania, Uganda, Rwanda and Kenya, Misha was responsible for coordinating activities between these countries and Denmark. This role took her to Denmark, Tanzania and Uganda.

Misha says she didn't always have a global mindset, but all that changed in her 20s when she discovered AIESEC at her university. She says, "When I got on AIESEC I knew I just didn't want to stay in Kenya."

Her first global encounter was with AIESEC as she went to a normal high school in Kenya with no opportunity to meet other international students.

When she joined AIESEC, Misha was fascinated by young international interns who had left their countries, to come to Kenya to work and explore. Even more refreshing was the diversity of their ideas.

AIESEC also afforded her the opportunity to meet corporate people, attend events and various international conferences at a young age.

While at university, she got involved with community

development and entrepreneurship and was responsible for marketing.

Misha's first job at AIESEC was marketing an educational internship to the principal of a local school. This task led to the school receiving an American intern who taught the students English. She recalls how the principal was proactive to sign on to that AIESEC initiative because he believed in exposing and expanding the horizons of his students.

Misha went on to later market the project to another school. She is happy to say this project is still running and has seen many interns from across the globe over the years.

Her interactions with course mates from Latvia, Thailand, Venezuela, China and Mexico at the Copenhagen Business School also provided her a daily global context.

Misha says, "Marrying an international husband and studying international business drives her global outlook now."

Her key learning point along the way is, "Never give up, and never lose focus", because after university, her desire to go for a role in AIESEC Egypt didn't work out, and although Kenya Gatsby Trust was in the works, Ghana came up as her first international job as a national marketing manager for AIESEC.

To succeed globally, Misha says, "It is important that one learns how to use their unique selling points (USP). Having a winning personality is crucial, and so is being passionate, confident, engaging, outgoing, and maintaining relationships." Although Misha wanted to study biomedical science after high school, she changed to business studies, and her love for talking led her to a Marketing degree. Misha's key skill is being a good communicator, and her real strength is networking with people. She is particularly good at following up with contacts and maintaining relationships.

She encourages young graduates to get international exposure, experience diverse cultures and different industry sectors when they have the opportunity. Misha has experienced working with an NGO, Banking, and Advertising, where she worked on global brands like Coca Cola and Societe Generale Ghana (SG).

She believes in pulling your socks up, and at Stanchart, she was part of a team that was instrumental in expanding the bank's network of branches.

Misha's journey did not come without challenges. Professionally, she recalls how disappointing it can get when people said "no", when she was selling AIESEC's initiatives. On a personal front, she points out there were a few challenges with regards to raising personal funds to be able to do things and go to places in the past. This was difficult, but she never gave up and stayed focused.

Not speaking many languages - especially Danish - as that is the language of her new home, can be a challenge, but she is working on it.

Misha had to learn research skills and the importance of summarising one's findings quickly. Always learning, she hopes to improve on her technical skills, particularly on social media marketing analytics, as well as her analytical skills to interpret complex information.

Misha has a lot of advice for African graduates and graduates the world over, who want to pursue global opportunities.

"Explore opportunities at university, because you have the chance to start practicing early what you learn."

"Go on internships, if possible, international internships, and read widely."

"Use the Internet smartly to get more information and expand your worldview and have an overview of everything."

"Hone your research skills and know how concepts are applied, not just the definitions of these concepts."

Prithi Mascarenhas

PRITHI is one of the main inspirations for this book. I recall meeting her whilst I was studying for my Master's degree at the University of Surrey in the UK, from 2002 to 2003. She was on her undergraduate programme at the time, and we became friends quickly. Prithi came to my aid when I had to conduct telephone interviews for Tourist Boards across French speaking Africa, for my MSc thesis. She called and spoke to the right people on my behalf. I was grateful, yet embarrassed that my country Ghana has only French speaking neighbours, yet like the majority of Ghanaians, we could not speak the French language. I have since mastered a few phrases that has served me quite well on my travels.

I was fascinated by Prithi's language skills, as well as all the places she had lived in and the many countries she had visited. She would say things like, "Italy will love you, and you will love Italy," or "You look like some of the models I booked in France." I had no clue then, as I had not travelled to many places, apart from growing up in Nigeria and going to England to visit my parents often (thankfully, today I have been to nearly 30 countries and the list is growing yearly).

Prithi has always been open to new experiences, and in no particular order, she has lived in India, Australia, France, UK, Spain, US and Austria. She has travelled to parts of

Africa, most of Europe, parts of Australia and South East Asia. From all these places, she has learnt that, essentially, people are the same everywhere.

Although Prithi originally considered a career in Finance, she is currently an HR manager for one of Europe's well-known CEOs. She says setting up the HR function in a business in a stand-alone role is her greatest career highlight.

Getting into the role was very competitive: she had to start at the bottom and get practical experience first. Naturally, as an HR person she has learnt that it is very important to build relationships with people.

Her first global encounter was probably via her very large and very international family; from her aunt who has been a nun in Zambia for over 20 years, to other uncles, aunts and cousins who can be found in places like Italy, Portugal, France, India, Australia and the United States.

Being born in a place with a huge tourist presence has influenced her thinking in a global direction. With her line of work, Prithi's global collaborations have been in the form of several meetings and conferences for work. She has observed that different cultures have their own collective styles and interactions in business, and cultural awareness is important when working with different people.

On having a global outlook, she says, "I think it is important to strike a balance between the global and local in every sense. In essence a 'glocal' outlook - if I may use the word, is probably more beneficial. I think being global in one's outlook is the bigger picture, but the local and traditional have a lot to bring to the global table."

Prithi is also inspired by the increasing and apparent

interdependence and connectedness across the globe. She contemplates if this trend was always the case, but asserts that, technology has made such connections and transactions a lot quicker and more transparent.

To be successful globally, Prithi says that success, to her, is a very personal word and she is still striving to be successful. But she thinks that being open to learning new things is the key to succeeding anywhere, whilst never losing your individuality and identity. Prithi wants to be able to celebrate diversity in a global context where, "We can all share and participate in each other's experiences."

Prithi can often see the bigger picture, which brings out her natural leadership qualities and confidence to deal with people and situations outside her comfort zone, and that is a solid quality and attitude she brings to the table. In addition to these, a combination of self-belief and humility are the constant attitudes she exhibits every time.

In spite of the above, she had to learn quickly how to be less modest and be able to sell her skills-set in a professional environment.

Moving forward, she would like to demonstrate more of her organisational skills.

Some of the challenges Prithli faces as a result of being in a global environment are: "The fast pace of life, and brief encounters with people and change."

If she is hiring a recent graduate, which she does often, she looks out for a personable individual who is willing to learn and has a proven academic record with extra-curricular interests.

Her advice for all graduates across the globe is, "Try

to get to know yourself first, to understand what you really want from life. Look at every opportunity as a stepping stone along the way to achieving your dream."

As to whether she would like to do anything differently, she says, "I wouldn't change a thing. That is not to say I haven't made mistakes, but I would not have learnt the lessons if I hadn't tried and failed."

Saulius Kubertavicius

With Saulius in Lithuania

AS a marathon runner who is also keen to climb mountains and explore the outdoors, I expected to see different kinds of training gear at Saulius's home, but instead it was a different story. When Saulius hosted me in his apartment in Kaunas during my visit to Lithuania to interview him, I felt I was back in Ghana. This is because he had pretty much 'carried' Ghana with him back home: local fabrics, art pieces etc. For a long time, Ghana was his second home, and after he had discovered all the corners of the country, he invited 17 other Lithuanians to join him on a road trip to explore Ghana and other parts of West Africa.

Prior to Ghana, he had previously worked in the US through a special program for students: Work and Travel USA, granting the opportunity to work for four months with a special J-1 visa and travel for another 30 days before leaving the country. During his Master's studies, Saulius also worked in an HR consulting company - Baltic Personnel Strategy Project Ltd.

Saulius came to Ghana on an AIESEC internship and one year quickly turned to five-and-a-half years working for Auto Parts Ghana, Nissan's distributor in Ghana. As AIESEC internships give young people the opportunity to access diverse experiences in over 100 countries, his goal at the time was to go far from home to experience a different culture. Saulius's internship was linked to his educational background in Human Resources, and he agrees it was a good extension for what he did.

At Auto Parts Ghana, he moved through various strategic roles: Training for front-line staff, Customer Service, Quality Management, and then as an After-Sales Manager.

When Nissan International was going through changes on a global scale, with the direction of promoting operational standards and customer service, this meant he had to step up and coordinate activities with the office in Japan, the regional head office in South Africa, Ghana and across the world.

Saulius had to represent the Ghana dealership by attending regional conferences organised by Nissan in Uganda, South Africa, Mozambique and Mauritius.

Saulius says his greatest experience was five years at Auto Parts Limited, the Nissan dealership in Ghana. At

Nissan, he learnt that business operations could be standardised: yet you can combine the mandatory, and have room and freedom to be creative in a regional context, and still find ways to adjust to the local market.

Saulius is currently a general manager for a trading company involved in personal safety and protective gear, a role he was invited to come back to Lithuania to explore, whilst still working in Ghana.

Connecting the dots, Saulius thinks he always had a global mindset, as he was always interacting with students from different countries during his years at university. He also made the effort to visit the USA on a work placement programme. Saulius has subsequently taken yearly trips to different countries, to broaden his horizon.

His global outlook is driven by what the opportunity of 'being global' creates. His philosophy is three-fold:

- Run quicker
- Run longer than your competitor
- Know the shortcuts and go the way others are not going. In a nutshell, know the environment.

Saulius points out that since the world is not just about the town or country you are in, "It is important to experience other countries and know that when it comes to development, there is always one country behind. There is one country waiting for your skills, if it is not happening in Ghana, go to Liberia, Togo or Sri Lanka or if you're late for Ghana go somewhere else, as most countries are all aspiring to a similar path."

Saulius's global journey began when as a child in 3rd - 4th grade, he was curious about the Danish couple renting a room in his family's apartment. They looked like him, but spoke a different language. His first global encounter was in 8th grade, when his school was invited by a Swedish NGO to take part in a youth festival in Sweden. It was a concert for children, where he learnt a lot of new things. He recalls seeing the very things he experienced in Sweden back home 10 to 15 years later. That was a wake-up call.

Some of the skills he has brought to the table include organising business operations, and customer orientation. As a child he was always organising something: beads, plates, books... organising and learning along the way always.

Saulius thinks hard work has helped him to succeed so far, and the plan is to become a market leader. But at this point in his career, he is learning a lot of new things and he particularly likes managing teams and running a company.

As a perfectionist and an idealist, he says he could learn the skill of delegating more in the future.

One crucial challenge he observed while working in a global environment is the cultural differences: particularly people who do what they want to do when they feel ready to do so, and are not necessarily focused on a delivery time or deadline. In other words it becomes a situation of different timing for everyone, not based on the task.

A global graduate to him is, "A person who finishes school knowing that he can realise himself in any country in the world." But, he quickly points out, "That requires a lot of effort."

His advice to students and graduates is to, "Leave their

own country for a year to know themselves and the world better. Just go do it." Saulius did just that and this has set him up for a remarkable career.

Saulius also encourages young people to pursue careers they like and be curious about whatever they are a doing. Ultimately, they must have self-belief.

Eva-Maria Olbers

NOT many people can say they have been to Easter Island or crossed the ancient Silk Road from Turkmenistan to Kazakhstan, driving 2000 km overland and mostly through dessert. Not many people I know take a long train ride for 3 weeks from Russia, through Siberia to China. But, Eva is used to doing the extraordinary. She goes on the most exciting adventures to fuel her curiosity and learning spirit. Even more remarkable, is the fact that Eva was able to do some of these exciting things, when she was a Consultant focused on Strategy Consulting for the high profile Boston Consulting Group in Munich, Germany.

Eva is from Luxembourg and Germany and has worked in 6 countries so far: in Private Banking in Luxembourg, in Global Banking in Spain, in Foreign Direct Investment Advisory in China. More short-term, she has also worked as an English teacher in India and as a microfinance project leader in Ghana.

She recalls her greatest career highlight so far to be her internship in China. She says of the experience, "It may not have been at the most prestigious company and I certainly did not earn a high salary, but I felt like I had direct impact with the work I was doing, that I had personal responsibilities and I had the joy of making myself understood in an entirely different business culture."

Eva studied International Business for her undergraduate degree at University of Warwick and did ESADE (Erasmus year abroad). At the Master's Level, she studied Management at London Business School. Eva maximized her opportunities by learning foreign languages (Spanish, French and Mandarin Chinese).

While in business school, Eva says, "My career considerations were quite defined, and to some extent perhaps even narrow-minded: I thought that the two major options for a business graduate would be either banking or management consulting – I myself started in consulting in the end. But as you gain experience and perspective, you realize how many more options are out there, some of which might have a better fit for you and even translate into more personal meaningfulness. Now I am considering different career tracks, such as working for a start-up, working for an international organization in the private or public sector or perhaps even starting my own company. As one develops, career options develop as well and make us grow professionally."

Eva has since joined Knewton, a tech and educational start-up and she is based in London.

Having lived in, studied at and travelled to a number of countries, this simply means there might be a lot of lessons to share from these countries. Eva confirms, "Each of them has taught me their own lessons for life – the particularities of each culture, the different day to day activities in people's lives, and the central role of religion. But most of all, I have learned that despite all the particularities, people are not that different in different parts of the world and you will find the kindest and most hospitable strangers no matter which country you are in."

Eva always knew the aspects of what was important to her on a job: working directly with people in an international environment, and working for a cause she believes in.

She outlines the main lessons from her past jobs:

"I learnt that it is all about people. Of course, the company you work for and what you do is important. But ultimately, the people you work with every day will influence your thinking and even well-being, both positively and negatively. So I learned that a hardworking and collaborative colleague can inspire and motivate you. At the same time an unsupportive boss can make you lose your motivation and perhaps, even the joy in what you are doing. That is why I tend to look at the people first before I chose a job or a company."

"I also learned that, you need to believe in what you do in order to be professionally fulfilled. The happiest young professionals I have met in my life were the ones who work in a field that made them feel passionate (for example, Arts) or people who are entrepreneurs. The unhappiest (and vast majority) were young people who saw the job only as a means to an end and were driven by external factors, such as a high salary or recognition by peers. They worked long hours without having an intrinsic motivation to do so. Sometimes this will be necessary in every young professional's career. The key is to learn how to step aside every once in a while and ask oneself whether this is something one really wishes to spend years doing, because time is rare and passes quickly."

Before applying to Boston Consulting Group (BCG), Eva says, "Looking back, I think that I got into BCG by doing three things: First, by thinking of what my own strengths were and in which field I could potentially use them. Then by finding a profession and a company for which my skill set could be useful to, and by having a good impression of the people working there. And finally, by not over-preparing for the interview.

The application process was relatively competitive, but given the thought process I had gone through before, I was able to justify not only what I could bring to the company, but also, why I felt that I would personally be a good fit. I tried not to get too stressed out by all the interview tips and practices, but I rather focused on being myself and on establishing a good rapport with my interviewer. I believe that if you feel happy and confident with the role you are applying for, the rest will work out by itself."

Eva's global encounter started early in primary school.

She attended the European School in Luxembourg: a school where more than 20 nationalities studied side-by-side daily. Knowing what she knows now, she felt it was still a very protected environment and showed only a small, selected part of a much more global world. She says her first 'real' global encounter was "When I was 17 and left to go to China on my own. This was when I realized what a global world really means."

Eva believes that we are born with a certain global curiosity. After that, it really depends on how you develop it. She says, "I think that I have always had a global mindset, but the reason I was encouraged to develop this were my parents who always told me as a child that one of the most precious things in life is to be able to see the world. When I was a teenager the travel bug really started to bite me and I couldn't stop using any free day I had to go somewhere or meet people from different countries. At some point, I realized that in today's globalized world, it is also very beneficial to have a global mindset: To be interested in what happens around the world, to learn foreign languages and to be open to work in different countries is always an advantage."

One cannot help, but wonder if there was any one person, thing or situation that has influenced Eva's thinking in a global direction. To this she says, "First of all, that would be my parents who always encouraged me to learn foreign languages and to live abroad. Then it would be the educational institutions I attended which made it possible to do so. And finally, it would be every single day that I spent traveling. It sounds ironic, but the more you travel, the more you will continue seeking that global direction. And every single person that I met on my travels, whether they were a fellow backpacker or a local host, has been my greatest inspiration to this date. The author of this book is one of them."

Eva's global collaborations are equally diverse; a piano concert of the Russian Federation in Luxembourg, the Duke of Edinburgh's Association at her secondary school, and the Emerging Markets Club at London Business School. She shares that "All of these collaborations brought young people together and encouraged them to work and create something together. The key learning points are vast and too many to list but they are valuable in an individual way to each participant."

Eva's global outlook is driven by her belief that, "Our future will become more and more global. You never stop learning if you think globally and surround yourself with international people: your horizon will only become broader. Of course you cannot always 'have it all', which is why it is important to find out what really is important for you. For me, the chance to lead a global life has always been a priority. I therefore don't really care about a nice apartment, car or clothes, but rather focus all my energy and also financial means to reach my personal goal of being able to see the world and meet new people. A global outlook for me means constant excitement and the hope to have an impact beyond national borders."

It is difficult to even imagine whether Eva has missed any opportunities as a result of not being strategically global in her outlook at any point in her journey. So I asked if she has. She says, "My spontaneous answer to this question would have been yes, I missed out on a global opportunity by moving back to my native country, Germany, to start my first job while I could have explored and learned from a new country and culture. However, looking at the question again, I noticed an important word in the sentence: 'strategically'. And this is why I need to reconsider my answer: While I always encourage people to live and work globally as much as possible, I believe that one should never ignore one's roots and norms. Having lived, studied or worked in your home country – having integrated and adapted in your own country's context – will help you develop that outward-oriented view in the first place and use it in a strategic way. It also looks good to employers if you show that you know and understand your own country first."

To succeed globally, Eva says it only takes a few things: "to be open-minded, to be tolerant, and to embrace change. To stop hesitating, pack a backpack and just try it. I promise you will not regret it."

Eva is modest in her response to what she brings to the table. She says, "I don't bring more to the table than anyone else. The only thing that I perhaps do differently sometimes is that, I don't only think about all the dangers and risks involved when going to a new country, but rather the experiences and people I could miss out on meeting. When I talk about living, working or traveling to a new country, most people ask me "Will you go alone?", "Isn't it dangerous?" and "Why on Earth are you doing this?". The answers are often "Yes", "Not if you act smart and know how to take care of yourself" and "Because these countries are there and exploring them and their people will be something I will learn from and benefit from for life. The only difference is that people are too hesitant to go, too scared of every possible outcome and reluctant to change. They ask too many questions and spend time holding themselves back while they should only be doing one thing: Just go."

In a global environment, the number one skill that has always helped Eva, is to be extroverted and to approach people. Eva suggests, "That is how you really meet the locals and establish contact with the country. The second skill – and this goes hand-in-hand with the first – is to listen to these people and to try to put yourself in their position. Everyone has fascinating stories to tell and if you give them a chance, they will share them with you."

On this global journey, the skills and attitudes she had to learn fast, include: "How to act politely when staying with Tibetan nomads, how to avoid any dangerous encounters in rural India, and how to dress appropriately as a foreign woman in Iran. What do all of these have in common? I had to learn quickly how to adapt to a local culture and how to keep myself safe. That is the most important thing."

Moving forward, Eva would like to focus on the important things at all times, and the attitude to be happy and grateful every day for what she has, instead of pressuring herself about unimportant things.

When it comes to the challenges of being in a global environment Eva says, "The more global your life is, the more challenging it is to maintain a stable and well-known base, because you are constantly moving. As I mentioned before, I believe that having some connection and roots to one's home country is essential. But much more importantly, it is crucial to not only build but also maintain personal relationships with family, friends and a partner. That can be challenging at times when a global environment is important to you – but even more fulfilling if you manage to combine it with the people most important in your life."

For Eva, "A global graduate is not someone who has travelled a lot. It is not even someone who has been to a foreign country at all. To me, a global graduate is someone who has the curiosity and the willingness to be global in his or her career. And if I were hiring a recent graduate, that would be exactly what I would look for: his or her international curiosity, worldview, and eagerness to learn and make something happen both within his or her own country and beyond."

If she were to give advice to a recent graduate from Africa, "I would tell this person to set no limits to him or herself ever. I would tell this person to choose a job they like and to mingle with everyone in a new country. And to tell everyone about their home country and their identity, tell them what it is like to be from East or West Africa, from a small African country versus a big country. Their contributions to any discussion will be extremely valuable and people from every continent are curious to find out more."

If she had to do it all over again, Eva says she would do some things differently. For instance, she "would always try to work in a field where I think I can contribute most. Someone once told me "Always compete with your strengths, never your weaknesses." I understand now what that person meant. And I wouldn't urge myself as much to comply with society's expectation. Do what makes you happy, not what others expect of you."

In the near future, Eva will look for a job where she can use her strengths. Although, she does not know what exactly that job would be, Eva is keeping her antennae up. What she does know is that, it will be a role where she can have an impact in a field that she believes in. Eva says, "Increasingly I realize that this might mean that I will move from the business sector towards my passion for international development, or perhaps even combine the two. I once read that the best way to predict the future is to create it. That applies to everyone. Don't let your fear of failing prevent you from trying, and…get started." I totally agree. We all just have to give our limited edition lives a shot.

Kweku Darteh Anane-Appiah

KWEKU spends his day managing the activities of a busy CEO who runs an energy company and a related chain of businesses. He spends his evenings pursuing his own fledging enterprises; a fashion design and styling studio, and a knowledge management venture.

Some of the possible career paths Kweku considered were Journalism, Public Relations and Advertising. He finally gave in to Advertising and Print Publishing, before moving onto other exploits. Human Resources Management was another fleeting interest he considered: this was precipitated by a short but interesting internship with an impressive professional who later became a close friend and mentor (reference to the author).

I wanted to know if Kweku always knew what he wanted to do. He answers: "Yes and no. Yes in the sense that I grew up fully aware of my natural inclinations towards the Arts; Communications, Journalism, Fashion Design, Advertising and Performing Arts Management. No because, I couldn't put a finger on just one area. I held a crazy fantasy to be an actor on Broadway, but I didn't have the guts to pursue it when I was younger – but I still have that particular fantasy notched away for later."

Kweku holds a BA in English, with a concentration in Literature and Sociology from the University of Ghana. He shares an interesting detail on how he disliked Sociology but later graduated to appreciate the discipline when thrown into the gruelling field of work.

He is also about to finish his Post Graduate Diploma in Business Administration, which focuses on Entrepreneurship, from the Graduate School of Governance and Leadership (accredited by the Kwame Nkrumah University of Science and Technology in Ghana).

Kweku reflects that getting into his current role was somewhat automatic: he had done his research and showed up with solid references and relevant transferrable skills acquired from over a decade of volunteering and work experiences. Prior to working for the CEO and his group of companies, he:

- Worked for an Educational Consultancy, where he was an admissions consultant for prospective US or UK bound undergraduates.

- Started his own company, Beeziminds, a knowledge management start-up that somehow failed to live pass its first attempt; nevertheless, Kweku assures me he is hard at work on a re-launch.
- Consulted and managed the Organizational Development Plan for American Field Service (AFS) Ghana: a partner of the AFS International fraternity of global experts in Intercultural Exchanges. At AFS, he also doubles as the Secretary to the Board of Directors and a member of the African Pool of Trainers. I found this impressive as Kweku joined the organisation in his teens to experience the diverse intercultural exchanges on offer.
- Managed the Business Development Section of PTL Solar Ghana; a local subsidiary of the parent company PTL Solar based in Dubai.
- Managed the operations and work traffic of jobs and projects for a small boutique print and outdoor advertising company.
- Interned for the Institute for Democratic Governance; a public policy think-tank, as a Programs Unit Intern during his National Service.

His greatest career highlight was when he was selected to join the first batch of AFS African Pool of Trainers. He says, "It took over 10 years to nurture my skills and competence towards this feat. I initially started out as an orientation facilitator, after which I learnt and perfected the trade and language to move up the ranks to earn this additional role within the international organization."

The next thing for Kweku is getting his companies Beeziminds and Queicoo's off the ground and running.

A combination of the good, the bad and the ugly lessons he gained from his past roles that he knows will guide him for future roles includes:

"Always leave your previous employment without drama, even if you're not treated fairly: the world is too small and interconnected to ruin a prospective deal caused by a disgruntled ex-boss."

"Be adamant about your 'non-negotiables', right from the start of a new job, or lose yourself and contentment in the process."

"Be proactive and go overboard with the expectations of your clients and bosses."

"You are dispensable: there is another young and exuberant version of you waiting to take your place, unless you constantly keep yourself and your skills-set relevant."

Spending a year in France as an exchange student was his first global encounter. He was 17 with a vivid imagination and great expectations of life. France made him discover himself without the distractions and influence of his family.

Kweku's global outlook is driven by international fame and connections: he wants to make a difference in the world and not just in his community and country. And his global perspective has been influenced by his affiliation with AFS and its core mission to create a world of peace, global understanding and tolerance through intercultural exchanges. He says, "There's no way you can volunteer for this cause without altering your views on the differences in cultures and people: somehow you become more open to multiculturalism."

He always had a global mindset as a child, and always thought of working and constantly travelling abroad. Though Kweku is from Ghana, he has had brief stints working (one-week long), in Kenya; participating in the EURAFRICAN Partnership project with AFS and the European Federation for Intercultural Learning (EFIL); and in Hungary, to offer a presentation themed 'Africa in Black and White' at the AFS Volunteers Summer Summit (VSS). He has also travelled to Germany, Austria, Dubai, Egypt and the USA.

The global collaborations he has been involved in include:

- AFS African Pool of Trainers TOT, Participant in Cairo, Egypt 2014
- European University Agents Meeting in Munich, Germany 2013
- Global Leadership Course, Summer Institute for Intercultural Learning Participant in Portland, USA 2013
- AFS Annual Volunteer's Summer Summit as a Trainer/ Participant in Zanka, Hungary 2011
- EURAFRICAN Partnership for Change Project, as a Participant/Trainer in Nairobi, Kenya and in Vienna, Austria 2011.
- AFS 80th Anniversary as a Youth Host Committee Member in New York City, New York 2007.

The key learning points from these collaborations, he admits, lies in the fact that "I am intelligent enough to sustain the interest of people of different colours and backgrounds, contrary to popular myths amongst many in Ghana." He strongly believes he can do all things through Christ who strengthens him.

Some of the challenges he has faced within the global working context include cultural misunderstandings and miscommunication, which at times comes across as intolerance and cultural disrespect.

On what it takes to succeed globally, and how he has done it, Kweku mentions, "Commitment, dedication, consistency, drive and confidence. I think I am well on my path, but nowhere near the finish line." Also, being open-minded, culturally sensitive to others, as well as being able to cross-culturally communicate, has given him an edge over others. He however had to learn communication and negotiation skills very quickly.

A global graduate, he says is:

"Someone who is exposed to varying cultural contexts and can easily switch social cues to effectively communicate cross-culturally."

"Someone who has honed their skills towards global relevance, and thus can interview and work anywhere across the globe."

"An avid reader, who is socially aware of global trends and issues and can eloquently discuss the respective issues with others confidently."

If he were to hire a recent graduate, he would look for the skills and attitudes outlined above.

Kweku's advice for the African graduate is, "The world is your oyster if you decide to overcome the mental boundary of inequality caused by race and or colour. Nothing can stop us from turning our reality around, should we invest into the right virtues, skills and conduct without fail or distraction."

I asked if he would change anything from the past, but Kweku says he will do it all over again, except take the Baccaulearaut in France and pursue a BFA in Acting and Directing at the University of Bordeaux. Moving forward, he plans to learn Cantonese and Spanish in addition to improving his cross-cultural negotiating skills.

Cristina Dandu

CRISTINA is a highly talented world-class freelance designer and illustrator, and there could be a great possibility that you might have seen or worn one of Cristina's award-winning designs for the popular clothes store Gap USA or Canada.

From an early age, Cristina says, "I really enjoyed drawing, but life has taken me in different directions. Sometimes it takes time and some life experience to realise something you knew all along." Cristina just completed a three-year

Animation Program in Ottawa, Canada. She also has a Bachelor's Degree in International Business and Commerce from The Academy of Economic Studies in Bucharest, Romania, her native country.

Cristina has had quite a number of different roles in the past 10 years. She started as a Client Service Executive in an advertising agency where she was in charge of the Client-Agency relationship concerning different advertising campaigns. She then moved to focus on a more creative role: copywriting for advertising, which meant writing every piece of text you see in an advertising ad, flyer, brochure or commercial. Both of these were in Bucharest. Cristina then tried a Marketing Executive role in Ghana and Dubai and became Art Director in two of the biggest advertising agencies in Dubai.

Cristina has not only worked in Romania, Ghana, United Arab Emirates (Dubai), but also in Egypt, Malta and Canada. She has also travelled for holidays in Bulgaria, Greece, Austria, Slovenia, Hungary, The Netherlands, Turkey, Oman, Jordan, USA, Thailand and Sri Lanka. She learnt a lot from these places, and about herself, from every single country she has been to. The main learning point from working in these places is to keep an open mind and learn to adapt to different situations. She says, "When working with different cultures, you have to take into consideration the cultural influences, be tolerant, and ready to adapt. And be nice. Always be nice. Never burn bridges, because you never know when you will meet that person again, or karma's gonna get you."

One of the main things Cristina stresses on, is to

appreciate life and the diversity it offers. She has also found it is not hard to relate with people from different countries, if you are honest and listen to them. As a result of this positive attitude, she has met great people everywhere she has been, and she still keeps in touch with many of them.

Cristina recognises that there are always challenges, no matter the environment: challenging tasks, high expectations and difficult people, and one would have to be more sensitive to cultural differences and be more aware of how those differences manifest in people's work ethic and way of approaching different tasks. Her own biggest challenge has been letting go of her own conditioning and misconceptions at times. In spite of these, Cristina's global outlook is driven by the fact that she really appreciates diversity in customs, ideas and opinions, and believes there is so much to learn from each and every culture.

As a freelancer, her role is not really a traditional one, but she is aware there is always going to be competition in her field of work and, this is not something she loses too much sleep over. Instead, she affirms, "You should care about finding something you love doing and getting really good at it."

Cristina knows every experience teaches you something. Some of the most important lessons are as follows:

"Listen to your heart; do what you want to do. Don't mind what other people think you should do. You are the one living with yourself day after day, so it's important that you are happy."

"You have to get used to working hard to get to where you want to be. Slackers and those who think they know a shortcut won't get too far in life."

"Allow yourself to make mistakes. Allow yourself to try different things until you find your way."

"It's never too late to do what you want to do. Time flies anyway, so why not make it count."

"Don't compare yourself to other people. Allow yourself to be inspired by what other people have achieved, but don't compare, because everyone has their own journey."

"Always remember great things take time. Don't expect quick results. Be ready to put in the hours and make sacrifices."

"Have a positive attitude towards life and learning. Always be open to new ideas, and don't be afraid of change."

"And here is a bonus one: Choose your friends wisely and try to surround yourself with people who both inspire and support you. It makes a world of a difference."

Cristina's first global encounter was back in the year 2000, during her first year of University. She joined the largest student organisation in the world, AIESEC. It was a very international environment, and that is when she had the chance to interact with people from other countries. She recalls it as a great time of learning and making new friends. AIESEC influenced the way she thinks in many ways, thinking globally being one of them. Through AIESEC she also realized she was the one controlling her experiences, and not the other way around.

She says, "My global mindset started forming while I was part of AIESEC, and since then I have always looked at myself as a citizen of the world, rather than just my own country."

Although she has been fortunate to work in many

countries, Cristina thinks the idea of personal success is a very subjective one. She believes that some of the attributes she has deployed in being successful, are: hard work, being persistent, pushing your limits, having an overall positive outlook on life, never limiting oneself, thinking, and remembering you can achieve anything if you focus on it hard enough.

Cristina tries not to compare herself too much with other people to find out what edge she has over them, but something that has helped her is the fact that she is hard working, imaginative and positive. Having that kind of outlook about life, together with a sense humour, are her go-to skills and attitude every time.

Cristina has also had to learn how to be organised and juggle different jobs at the same time. She believes being organised with your work and life is a big plus.

In her profession, she learns every day and believes that in order to be a great professional, you have to push yourself to learn new things all the time, whether by reading blogs, talking to different people, going to conferences, or taking courses. She advises, "Never be complacent, but always strive to improve yourself."

Moving forward, Cristina is working on having a more balanced life. This she says is hard, but not impossible, especially when you want to achieve a lot of things.

The main thing that Cristina will look out for when recruiting a recent graduate is passion. That passion she says, "Translates into seeing that person being proactive, getting involved in projects related to what they want to achieve and being willing to work hard. I like to see energy, resourcefulness and confidence. Attitudes like "Oh, I could not get a job because everybody expects experience" or "I wanted to do…. but didn't have the time," just sound like excuses to me and tells a lot about someone's outlook on life and work."

Her advice to other graduates is, "To think big! Don't compromise on what you want to do just because you had people telling you, you can't or you shouldn't. I would say be brave when approaching life, and don't be afraid of making wrong decisions or mistakes, because those will just serve as lessons and most probably great stories down the road. Always remember it is all one big journey."

Cristina does not focus on what could have been, but rather tries to focus on, "What is and what it could be." Hence, she cannot recall if she has missed any opportunities along the way. If she had to do it all over again, Cristina says, she would probably spend a bit more time in Ghana, but she plans to return.

Next on Cristina's list, is building her own studio after finishing animation school. And for someone whose designs have been internationally recognised by Gap USA and Canada, as well as having other international clients appreciating and requesting her work, I have no doubt that her designs will win more awards, be splashed across the globe, and her studio will do well.

Mark Calzaverini

MARK is from 'many places', and speaks several languages with perfect accents. He is English and, Italian and grew up in Spain.

His first global encounter would probably be when he did a French language summer course in France. He was 14 years old and met people from around the world.

Mark has travelled to most countries in Europe, as well as to Singapore, Thailand, Hong Kong, Brazil, Argentina, Uruguay, US, Turkey and Tunisia. He has learnt from every travel experience: the way people live, the things they do, and their culture. In the end he realised that, no matter how different we all are, we have a lot of things in common.

Although Mark always had a global mindset, he says, "It is a very difficult thing to define, because, in my case I can say I am always the one making an effort to adapt to the other person's mindset, culture and even language. I was also very good at geography at school. Name any country in the world and I can tell you the capital and where it is located." This is very true, because I recall meeting Mark about 11 years ago and when he knew I was from Ghana, he immediately told me Accra was the capital and followed that up to show me Ghana on a world map on his wall. This was quite impressive, as I had had an earlier encounter, where someone asked me, "Which was bigger, Ghana or Africa?" I was horrified, to say the least.

About the beginning of his career, Mark says, "I was just trying to survive. I don't regret anything, but my decision to work abroad for a few years has had a negative effect on my career progression. This is because the online advertising market in the UK is fiercely competitive and much more advanced than continental Europe. This makes it difficult for outsiders to succeed."

Mark's past roles includes working for a start-up in London, a travel portal in Paris, an e-tailer in Paris, and an agency in Barcelona.

He acknowledges that you learn with every experience. Although he has learnt so many things along the way, his summary is, "I have learned to be professional."

Mark is currently an Account Manager for an affiliate

network in London. Although he considered careers in Advertising and E-commerce, he always knew that he wanted to work in a commercial role for an Internet company.

He has a BSc (Hons) Computing & IT from the University of Surrey, Guildford-England, and a Postgraduate MSc in International Management from Royal Holloway, University of London.

Getting into his current role was competitive, and he had to use a recruiter and five interviews to get the job.

Mark's global collaborations include dealing with publishers and clients that are based in places like Dubai, San Francisco and Sydney. He is modest and mentions, "But this is a pretty common thing these days." In the past, Mark also travelled between London and Paris a lot, for work.

The key learning points for him during these collaborations, particularly when he used to travel Paris-London-Paris, he says, "I would often find myself in situations where I was the middleman interpreting and translating not only words, but an entire different way of working, and culture, between countries. That is quite a challenge, and it forces you to learn much about the nuances of what people say and what they really mean." In his current role, it is more about ensuring that you work around the different time zones. He points out, "For example, if you work with the US, you have to e-mail them in the morning so you will see their replies coming in later in the afternoon."

Mark's global outlook is driven by the Internet, because it has changed everything for many businesses. He shares his insights by saying, "If you think about it, it makes total sense. We are now living in a day and age where, if something happens in Fiji or Costa Rica, the rest of the world will know about it in an instant. If you stop and think about it, it is absolutely fascinating. Never in the history of humankind was this possible. Also, air travel... Think how, for example, the way Columbus travelled to the Americas over 500 years ago, venturing into the unknown, and compare that with how you or I can purchase a plane ticket online and fly across the world with such ease (comfortably in first class if you have the money)."

On one hand, Mark's most valuable attitude is perseverance. Regarding the other skills and attitudes he brings to the table that makes him have an edge over others, Mark says, "I try to bring a very personal approach to everything I do. As an Account Manager, you help your clients by anticipating problems and acting as their "consigliere", in Mafia speak."

On the other hand, the skill and attitude he had to learn fast in his current job, is the need to constantly balance good quality work with fast work. Mark would also like to be a lot more technical in his work.

For him, the challenge of being in a global environment is that you do not know where the next big thing will come from. This is why it is key to constantly learn new skills and maintain a competitive edge.

Mark thinks anyone can be a global graduate, "As long as he or she is aware of the fast-paced, 24 hour ultra-capitalist, boundary-less world we are living in." If he had to hire a recent graduate, he would find someone with a can do attitude, a team player with Maths and language skills who also has a basic understanding of the Internet.

His general advice to all recent graduates, no matter where they are from is: "Get a job and learn or start your own business and learn."

If he had to do it all over again, Mark thinks, he would have most likely done a lot of things differently. However, he reflects, "But had I done that, I wouldn't be where I am today, so no. You cannot live your life full of regrets."

His next career move is simple, "Tomorrow morning I will wake up at about 7am or 7.30am and go to work. I will continue to build a future for myself and take my career forward."

Edwige Takassi

EDWIGE works for ProCredit Holding, a German company that created a group of banks specialised in very small businesses and SMEs in developing and transition countries.

She is currently assigned to ProCredit Bank in the Democratic Republic of Congo (DRC) as a Deputy General Manager. The bank in DRC has 450 employees and 17 branches; and it is also number 5 in terms of total assets, out of 20 banks.

Edwige is in charge of three main business areas:

- General risk management, including credit risk, operational risk and financial risk
- Front office operations, which includes the management of the quality of services in branches
- HR, which includes recruitment, administration and training

Although Edwige did not always know what she wanted to do, she did not want to be influenced by her parents' pre-established choice. This meant she did not really know where to seek guidance. In high school, she was interested in business management in general, and at this point she started having a clearer idea of her future career path during her studies.

Edwige studied Economics and also has a Master's degree with a specialisation in Banking and Audit. Some possible career paths she considered after her studies were working in Audit, Controlling and Banking. She applied to several companies in all of those areas, went through several rounds of interviews, and the first concrete opportunity was in banking, which is where she started.

She first worked for Societe Generale, a French international bank, in Paris. This was a contract in collaboration with the management school she attended, so that all her placements (12 months in total) were done with the bank. She says of the time, "This helped me finance my studies and learn all the important elements related to retail banking, as I went through front office positions from Cashier to Client Advisor, and Credit Analyst."

After she graduated, Edwige worked for a couple of

years in Audit for PricewaterhouseCoopers in Luxembourg. This experience gave her a good insight into the way companies work and are managed, including aspects related to internal controls, budgeting and planning, as well as financial statements review.

Once she thought she had enough experience in her field, she decided it was time to go back to Africa. She applied to international companies active in developing countries, specifically in areas related to development finance.

Edwige landed a role at ProCredit group after going through several rounds of competitive interviews, in which she performed extremely well. Her first assignment was as a Managing Director of ProCredit in Ghana, where she stayed for three-and-a-half years.

Below she outlines some of the good, bad or ugly lessons she learnt from her past roles that have prepared her for her current one:

The toughest was, "Hard work is key. Even when we have the feeling no one is watching, there always comes the evaluation day when a supervisor will check one's performance not just against expectations but also against other people's performance. Only the ones giving their best have a chance to move forward in a fair system. I learnt this the hard way because the very first evaluation in my career was bad, not because I was doing a bad job, but because other people were really taking it much more seriously than I did, and I missed an opportunity. So, first lesson is: make career plans and give your best to show you're serious about it. If you don't, no one will do it for you and you'll be outcompeted fast."

The second thing she mentions is what she terms 'philosophical lessons about work'. This is because, "You don't choose who you work with, unless you're the owner of the business, therefore there will be times when you're tempted to play the victim: My boss does not like me; my colleague is not a team player; my subordinate refuses to accept my authority, etc. There is no point playing the victim. It is important to analyse each situation, take a decision, and make the best out of it. Act upon the things you can change, and adapt to the things you can't change. Not every battle is worth fighting. The war is long and you'd better save your energy for the real important fights. I learnt this from people I call my mentors. They never really realised they were mentoring me, but in fact I observed the people I was looking up to and deduced from their behaviour, deeds and what they were saying. There were many things I wanted to incorporate into my way of thinking and behaving.

I also observed people I was really struggling with, and deduced many things I wanted to avoid in my way of thinking and behaving. I also learnt that anyone able to formulate criticism is useful, although our spontaneous reaction is often defensiveness. Very often, we learn things from criticism much more in fact than we do from praise. We should be able to question ourselves. No matter how tough it is formulated, criticism is useful, and it's free. It's up to us to do something constructive with it."

The third thing is, "I learnt that it is important to define standards for oneself. Professionalism, integrity, ethical standards are part of the things important to me. Standards are derived from values. Values should be taken seriously, and we should never compromise with our values."

Edwige says her greatest career highlight was, "Probably when I started training (people), I discovered I loved it and this was a completely new experience, adding diversity to my job."

Edwige is from Togo, and she is also a French citizen. She has lived, studied and worked in France. Apart from the DRC, Ghana, France and Luxembourg, she has also worked in Mozambique and Germany. Edwige has travelled to Cote d'Ivoire, Mali, Burkina Faso, Benin, Congo, Botswana, Zambia, Morocco, Tunisia, Italy, Spain, Portugal, The Netherlands, Austria, Turkey, Romania, Serbia, Croatia and Colombia. She did learn from every place she had been to. The lessons mainly are the understanding that, there are many different cultures and ways of living, and they impact the way people relate to, work with and socialise with each other.

Edwige says, she always had a global mindset and was equally attracted to and intrigued by other cultures. Her first global encounter was an indirect one: through her dad. She says, "I was very young, probably around five years old, and my dad used to travel abroad a lot for work. Every time he came home, he brought something back from wherever he had been. Sometimes they were books, sometimes a dress, sometimes just cookies or sweets, and I was so proud to know it was coming from far away, though I had no clue about the meaning of abroad. "

Her dad equally influenced her thinking in a global direction. He always spoke about the importance of travelling and speaking foreign languages.

Her global collaborations range from certain projects during her studies, like taking a course called cross-cultural management with about 10 different nationalities sitting around a table to work on a common project. The time she spent in Luxembourg, where she had to work in teams, always including people from 2 or 3 different countries, was key.

In her current work, she frequently attends international seminars with people from the 21 countries (representing 3 continents) her company works in.

Some of the learning points from these collaborations, she summarised as the concept of 'cross cultural management'. This is because communication and behavioural codes are different from continent to continent, and from country to country. When communicating, it is important to cross check if our message is understood the right way, and if both parties involved understand each other.

Edwige also learnt that performance standards can be different from country to country, even within the same company. And despite all these differences, very often, it is quite easy to learn things from each other, and it is worth trying different ways of doing things. She stressed, "Our default position tends to be 'This would never work in my country/culture, when in fact, in business, daring to try new things often creates opportunities."

Commenting on what it takes to succeed globally, and how she has done it, Edwige confesses, this is a very broad question and one that is difficult to capture in just a few words. But, she asserts, "It takes openness and hard work. It also simply takes time and patience." Her analytical skills, the ability to communicate in difficult and conflict charged situations are some of the key skills Edwige has brought to the table to have an edge over others, although she admits she had to learn public speaking very quickly.

Edwige's key challenge of being in a global environment, is not being able to understand everyone's language. Even though English is often spoken as a common language, she points out "expressing things in a language that is a foreign language for both persons sometimes dilutes things." And even though she speaks French, English, German and is learning Spanish, Edwige says she will love to learn more languages as well as learn to develop knowledge in psychology, with emphasis on a cross cultural/anthropology aspect. As a manager, she thinks this could be useful, because it will help her understand people's reactions and approach to solving problems.

To her, "A global graduate is someone who has lived and or studied in at least two countries and has been influenced enough by another culture to include lessons learnt into his or her daily life." If she is hiring a recent graduate, which she does all the time; she looks out for someone dynamic and curious: someone who is able to adapt to change and who shares some of her values.

Her advice for recent graduates about to step out into the world is, "Leave your social cage aside: it is made of useless prejudice. Discover other cultures and share your own."

If she had to do it all over again, will she do anything differently? Edwige says: "I am tempted to say yes, list my mistakes and say I should have known better. However, those mistakes are also part of what brought me to where I am today, so no, I don't think I would do anything differently."

Edwige is not planning to change jobs any time soon. However, since she has not yet developed all the sets of skills she wants to develop, the next step for her will be to upgrade her knowledge and competence in certain key topics, in order to build expertise in those areas.

Christian Eyoup

CHRISTIAN is Cameroonian. He has a Master's Degree in Management Control from Catholic University of Central Africa (Cameroon)/Catholic Institute of Yaoundé.

Christian always had an idea of the sectors in which he wanted to work. He saw himself either working in the Oil industry or in the Banking sector.

After his university studies, he thought of joining an audit firm, particularly one of 'The Big 4': PwC, E&Y, Deloitte & Touche or KPMG.

He however started as a Junior Auditor (learner/beginner) in a local Audit Firm after university, then went International to work with PwC in Ghana where he joined the

Crisis Management Department (Advisory Services) as an Advisor, for over 2 years. He then returned to Cameroon to work as a Financial Analyst in an Investment bank, BMCE Capital, which is the investment branch of the renowned Moroccan Bank, BMCE Bank.

Christian currently works with Union Bank of Cameroon. He joined the Foreign Department of the bank as a beginner, although he already had experience as a Financial Analyst for an investment Bank. He joined his current company in an attempt to integrate the banking sector, and he is responsible for Western Union and other transfer products.

The first thing he learnt from his past role, is to be pro-active. This is followed by the need to be curious about one's work, taking charge of your own personal development, and paying attention to detail. These lessons were all important and relevant for excelling in subsequent jobs.

Of his first ever global encounter, Christian says, "Definitely my first step with the international environment was working for PwC Ghana Ltd., because it was the first time for me to go out of my country and work in a multicultural environment."

He has also travelled to Morocco, Togo, Nigeria, South Africa, Benin, Kenya, Côte d'Ivoire, Germany, France and Belgium.

Being a French speaker and having spent all his life in a French culture, Christian's travels gave him the first life-time experience of the working habits of other non-French speaking countries and cultures.

Christian admits that in the beginning, he did not always have a global mindset, but after meeting with young students from various countries and continents, he decided, "I'll do my best to pay them a visit when I have the opportunity," so he could learn more.

AIESEC, the global organisation present in over 100 countries, influenced his thinking in a global direction, because it exposed him to various experiences, and he ultimately developed a myriad of skills.

Christian says he has been fortunate to be part of various global collaborations, with AIESEC, PwC and his current work. These collaborations have either been leadership conferences or meetings. The key learning points from these collaborations are: Respect for schedules (Time management); being organised and prepared in a business meeting; always anticipating others' needs and questions; and looking smart at all occasions, because getting the dress code right is very important.

Christian says his global outlook is driven by the desire to learn from others and exchange our experiences. He wants to challenge himself as well as compete with others so he will be able to bring on board something different to the table. He sees being multicultural as a big advantage, because the capacity to speak two or three different international languages is remarkable.

As someone who likes to be proactive, he does not recall missing any international opportunities as a result of not being strategically global in his outlook.

To succeed globally, Christian agrees that one needs a variety of skills in addition to being hardworking. He has consistently demonstrated these sets of skills. Christian says the edge he has over others is his ability to manage teams and supervise their work. He can also speak three languages: French, English and Spanish. Knowing French has always been a plus each and every time he is in an English speaking country, "It has opened so many doors," he adds.

His greatest career highlight, thanks to his French skills, was when he was able to recover close to one million dollars during a debt collection exercise.

In spite of his language skills, Christian had to learn fast and adopt a different attitude when it came to speaking and using English. This is because in the beginning, he had to really try to be as good as a native English speaker. He then needed to adapt to the working environment and working style, and learn a new way of time management.

Moving forward, the skills and attitudes he would like to learn or demonstrate more of, is to deliver neat jobs on time without typos, and be able to manage a team from the beginning of a project until the end, without hurting the feelings of others or generating misunderstandings.

According to Christian, some of the challenges of being in a global environment are, being alone most of the time, and at other times, having the feeling of not being understood. Also, things are not always done the same way as in one's own country and sometimes a lot is being asked of you.

In Christian's view, a global graduate is "Someone who can adapt and learn fast in a new environment: someone who has the will and the desire to succeed, and who never gives up, no matter what."

If he were hiring a recent graduate, Christian would look out for the working tools the person is familiar with, their extracurricular activities, and the roles they played.

His advice for his fellow Africans is: "Challenge is what makes you. Give your best, gain in maturity, and also understand the world in which we are living and growing. Never be afraid to compete with other ethnic groups, races, etc., because that's where you learn a lot and improve yourself, and sometimes you realise you are even better or equal to some extent."

To recent graduates, Christian's advice is on the need to make great use of your working tools, such as Microsoft Excel, PowerPoint, Word and Access, because they will put you a step ahead of others."

If he had to do it all over again, would he do anything differently? Christian says: "Of course, I will do it differently. I would prepare myself better and won't give space to ignorance."

His next career move is going back for international opportunities. He says, "I am well prepared and I know what is at stake."

Malcolm Azumah

Malcolm's greatest career highlight was in the army. He says, "I never knew I could function well out of my comfort zone, until I was deployed to Iraq." He now knows better not to underestimate the ability of the human brain in a survival mode.

Malcolm grew up in Ghana, where all he knew was to study science. He did not know where it would lead him, but he went ahead and studied Physics for his undergraduate degree at Kwame Nkrumah University of Science and Technology and a second undergraduate degree in Civil Engineering at Kingston University, Surrey, UK.

At this point, he was considering careers in Structural Engineering, the Military, Piloting, being an Event Coordinator, Entrepreneurship and many more.

Malcolm went on to start a Master's programme in Structural Engineering at the University of Surrey, but three months to completion, he realised it was not for him, so he left. Today he has finally found what he wanted to do and is pursuing a double major MBA/Actuarial Science at Ball State University in the USA.

Malcolm says, "I knew getting onto the MBA programme was always going to be competitive, especially when you don't have a clue, but once you know what you really want, it's just an easy step." As a former army man, he never underestimates the importance of having enough information to be prepared. This is a skill he uses daily.

Malcolm has worked and lived in the United Kingdom, Iraq, Qatar, Belgium, Germany and about five states in the United States of America. He has also visited Holland, Italy, Spain, Canada, France and Togo. From all these places he has learnt that being confident and having the right exposure is very advantageous. Because of his diverse exposure to other cultures and religious views, he is always selected to participate in international conferences, meetings and concerts in most parts of the world.

Malcolm's past roles include working as a freelance engineer in London, teaching Mathematics in high schools both in Ghana and London for almost 4 years, running a Non-Profit by proxy for a friend from Bangladesh, and Military Service with the British Army, where he was deployed out of UK and then as an office dispatch coordinator in California.

From all these roles he has learnt one thing: that having and knowing how the big picture is globally, regardless of being in a small office in a remote part of the world, is crucial.

Although he did not always have a global mindset in relation to work, he did when it came to going on holidays. In his travels, he found that he liked some places better than others, and he was on a quest to establish his life in a particular location. This forced him to understand the culture and the socio-economic intelligence needed to be able to survive wherever he finally decided on staying.

Malcolm's first global encounter was when he started

working with people outside his birth country Ghana. He says, "Understanding how the big picture fits globally, and the ability to be marketable not only in your birth country, but in other parts of the world, greatly influenced my career and lifestyle." Malcolm adds, "It is important to fit into any organisation and not be found wanting." He also suggests that knowing how a country (politically, socially and economically) is run on a day-to-day basis would impact greatly on one's productivity. He shares the importance of knowing and remembering the different time zones, when working on international projects.

Malcolm points out that before embarking on a global journey, one has to consider and understand the impact of one's global journey on their immediate family, as a balancing act can be challenging. This sense of awareness and opportunities also comes with some challenges. Malcolm says, "The pressure, fatigue, and financial strain it can have on a person made me appreciate the introduction of webinars and meetings via most of the global networks available."

Malcolm's global outlook is driven by the impact of knowledge accumulation and services to mankind. He is well aware of the challenges that come with competing with other equally good people from other parts of the world for the same great opportunities.

Malcolm has missed some opportunities in the past, because he was not strategically global in his outlook. In retrospect, he knows, "When you have no information on exactly what you want to do in life or you have no clear direction in life, you will miss so many opportunities." On a more personal level, he says, "I have lost 12 years of my life because I was in search of myself and what I wanted to do."

Although he lost 12 years trying to find answers, while at the same time finding more ways to have a competitive edge, his search paid off in the end. He has figured out what exactly he wants to do. Malcolm thinks it might be a lot easier for the new generation of graduates to succeed globally. This is because there are a variety of global programs, consultants and coaches available who have travelled the length and breadth of the world and are ready to inform and impact anyone who is willing to take it to the next level.

If he were to recruit a recent graduate for a job, he would look for a candidate who can answer among other things, strategic interview questions on how well they know about the company they have applied to, how the company operates globally, and if the candidates think they will be a good fit, and why. He would also want to know whether the candidate thinks about the bigger picture, and after the interview, whether the candidate would ask questions pertaining to the big picture, such as how, in their opinion the company is doing, compared to the rest of the world.

To get ahead, Malcolm had to quickly learn a lot of computer programming and software packages. In the future, he would like to learn and demonstrate more knowledge on foreign policies and global decision-making. To this he says, "If we think the decisions made in the White House do not affect some remote village in my hometown Sogakope, then I would be kidding myself. They do."

His advice to recent graduates is, "There are programs and courses that allow you access to other parts of the world.

Research into what you want to do; take relevant courses; attend conferences; understand some of the global 'jargon'; think outside the box; don't limit your analysis to your home countries alone; broaden your horizon; and be analytical. All these tell the person listening to you, "WOW". You always have the power to convince people, if you think outside the box of your country."

Malcolm says he would not change anything from his past, because, "as much as I don't like missing out on opportunities, I am also grateful for all the mistakes. It paved the way to advise the new generation so they can make it better than we did."

Sezen Oznacar

MEETING a foreign tourist one summer holiday while she was in her teens, was Sezen's first-ever global encounter. She became aware of the differences in their respective behaviours and mode of dressing. Leaving her teenage years behind, Sezen thinks the main quality of a global graduate should be open-mindedness, and with that kind of attitude, no matter where one is from they can achieve their goals.

Sezen is from Izmit, Turkey and is a Sinologist who has just relocated from Belgium to live in Doha, Qatar. Because she knew what she wanted to be, her career path has been a strategic one.

She first got an MA in Sinology from Ankara University,

Turkey, then an MBA in EU Business from EHSAL European University, Belgium, and a PG in EU-China Business Development. With her degrees and her job experiences as a corporate language trainer in Belgium, and a Business Development Consultant in China, she had the audacity to follow her dreams and set up a company as a Cross Cultural Communication Trainer and a EU-China Business Development Consultant.

Sezen has also travelled to France, Germany, Holland, Luxembourg, Spain, UK, USA, Cuba, Cayman Islands, Thailand and Egypt.

Sezen believes that, to succeed globally, one has to have a respect for differences and cultures, which sums up her definition of having a global mindset. She loves meeting people from different cultures and however difficult it is, she accepts everyone as they are.

Engaging in various networking events in China and her past work experience as a volunteer English teacher in China are instances that also encouraged her to adopt a global mindset.

The key learning point for her as a Volunteer English teacher in China in the evenings after her regular work, taught her that "money is not everything, but sharing experiences, knowledge and helping people to go further is great."

If she had to do it all over again, Sezen says she will do it differently, because 3 months after she arrived in Belgium, she wanted to be economically independent and began to work as an English teacher. As a result she had no time to learn the national languages and her inability to speak French and Dutch proved to be a major challenge when she wanted to find work after some years. In retrospect, Sezen says, she would not have began working as an English teacher; first she would learn both languages then begin to work. Regardless of these initial setbacks, she emphasized she still has no regrets.

When it comes to thinking about her future, she says, "I am not afraid and I do deeply believe that something good is waiting for me. I will do my best to get what I deserve. I would like to be one of the best cross-cultural trainers and, a well-known China expert."

Sezen's strongest points have been patience, hard work and courage. Being courageous is what gets her going the most, a trait she had to learn fast to survive.

Her greatest career highlight is succeeding against the odds when she relocated to Belgium. She says, "I left my country, family, friends and habits behind me and got married and moved to Belgium. I did not know anybody or anything about the culture or even a word in the Belgian national languages. To be honest, I did not know that it would be that difficult to have another nationality and be accepted for jobs. Indeed it was! But, I had no other choice than to succeed, so I continued to search, regardless of the setbacks with a positive attitude. I applied for many jobs by keeping in mind "never give up". I then decided to become a freelancer. It worked out very well. Thanks to my courage I succeeded very well. I am proud of what I have achieved 13 years in Belgium. I have trained hundreds of people with great feedback." Sezen hopes to repeat her success in Qatar – a new country, new culture and no knowledge of the language. She just hopes it is not as difficult as it was in Belgium.

For now, her plan and her attitude is to, "chin up, go a step further always, keeping in mind it is important to do my best even if sometimes it is not the best of others." This is not just a plan for Sezen, but, it is her mindset and her affirmative statement- one that has seen her through Turkey, Belgium, China and now Qatar.

Eric Kusoatsi

WITH his undergraduate degree in International Management from Rotterdam Business School in The Netherlands, and a Master's in International Business Economics from City University, London, some of the possible career paths Eric considered were: being an Advertising or Marketing Professional, an Economist, or a Management Consultant. Eric's interests changed as he tried out different roles in different companies and organisations.

His past roles have included:

- Account Manager (Advertising Agency – Accra, Ghana)
- Client Liaison Officer (Local Government – London, UK)
- Business Administrator (Executive Transportation Company – New York)
- Customer Service Advisor, Customer Service Supervisor, Team Leader (all with the same company)

Eric currently works as a manager in the Operations Department of a luxury online retailer that is based in New York. And even though he got into his current role as a result of an internal promotion, he had to distinguish himself to show that he was the right candidate for the role.

Eric shares some key lessons from his past roles that prepared him for his current role. Some of these lessons are:

- "Be professional in every aspect of the word: dressing, speaking and acting appropriately. Others will see you and treat you as such."
- "Be prepared to do more than is expected or required. Going the extra mile always gets you noticed."
- "Don't always ask for 'what's in it for me'? Rewards are not always instant, and they may not always come in the form of an instant salary increment."
- "Always ask questions and seek to learn, especially from those in more senior positions."
- "Whatever task you find yourself doing, try to do it to the best of your ability, while learning as much as you can."
- "Always take the initiative. If you're done with a particular task, always seek for more to do - or a better way to do something - and suggest it to your supervisor. This always gets you noticed."

Eric is from Ghana and has worked in four countries: Ghana, The Netherlands, The United Kingdom, and the United States. In addition, he has visited Togo, Benin, Burkina Faso, Nigeria, South Africa, Belgium, Luxembourg, Germany, France and Canada. Visiting, living and in some cases studying in some of these places gave Eric a couple of life lessons. The main ones are:

- "Everywhere, everyone is trying to make it."
- "Some countries create an environment where the tools and resources to learn and succeed are readily available. It is essential to take advantage of these resources where they are available."
- "The world is a competitive place and your success for the most part will depend on your own decisions plus external factors that are not within your control."
- "Just as no two neighbourhoods in a city are the same, no two countries are the same."

Eric's first close interaction with an international audience was being in a foreign language class in Belgium with other students from different countries; and learning a new language.

Eric points out that he did not always have a global mindset, but it developed over time as he was exposed to international cultures and environments through the books and magazines he read, or through international programs he watched. He says, "The encouragement of my parents to read – reading exposes one to a world beyond one's own reality - influenced my thinking in a global direction." Also, "The quest and need to be consistently relevant and up to date in today's global environment", is what drives Eric to be global in his outlook.

Some of his global collaborations are either in a volunteering capacity or taking part in United Nations Foundation's Young Professional Organisation events in New York (networking events, film screenings, talks and discussions, etc.). Eric has also attended a New York University

African Economic Forum, as well as The School of Oriental and African Studies (these are African-related programs in London, UK). To Eric, some of the benefits from these collaborations are:

- It broadens one's perspective about the world in which we live
- It makes you appreciate and work better with different cultures and people
- You learn about different cultures and people, and this makes you more informed and a better person
- It helps you think and act globally in this interconnected world
- There is value in meeting new people, networking and making connections.

I wondered if Eric has at any point missed out on any opportunities as a result of not being strategically global in his outlook. He says, "There have been some missed opportunities, such as not visiting or exposing myself to more countries or cultures, or not learning a new language when I had the opportunity to. However, it is never too late, and every recognized missed opportunity by itself is a chance to do something about it."

Eric has a lot of insight to share, when it comes to what it takes to succeed globally, and how he has done it. He reflects, "Success is not a finite position. It is a journey or process which has everything from mountains and valleys: some of them easy to climb, and others are more difficult. No success comes easy, and it doesn't happen overnight. The journey will have some setbacks and failures, and there will also be victories, some minor and others major, and everything in between." For Eric, it is important to enjoy the journey, a journey that entails:

- Constant learning
- Being open to and embracing change
- Not settling, but consistently challenging yourself and thinking how to keep improving and developing not only yourself but whatever it is that you are involved in and interested in
- Celebrating victories and learning from mistakes
- Sharing your experiences with others, and helping others along your way.

Eric points out that he does not have "one main edge" over others, but the key attributes that have helped him along the way, are to work hard and be open to learning. These qualities have never failed him. He compares that attitude with going to a gym and pushing yourself a bit more every time.

Not being content with the status quo, but thinking about continuous improvement, is the one useful attitude Eric exhibits every time. However, multitasking and managing change effectively were the skills he had to learn quickly. Moving forward, Eric is set on seeking the most effective ways to create value in everything he is involved in, or with those he comes into contact with.

In Eric's view, some of the challenges of being in a global environment are:

- Keeping up with the constantly changing landscape
- Keeping abreast with and sifting through the tons of available information
- Staying focused on tasks or goals that have been set, while other things always vie for your attention and involvement.

A global graduate, Eric says, is: "One who doesn't confine him or herself to the physical boundaries of where they are located or from what they learn, but one who seeks to and exposes themselves to a global environment, where they learn and apply that well-rounded knowledge effectively in every aspect of their lives."

If he were hiring a recent graduate, Eric would hire someone who has or can demonstrate the following attitudes and qualities:

- Attentiveness, open-mindedness and eagerness to grow and learn
- Focus and commitment
- Following instructions and yet open to asking questions
- Being a self-starter (i.e. taking initiative)
- Professionalism in every approach

Eric chose to share his very deep thoughts, insights and advice on various areas to recent graduates who are about to step out into the world from the African continent. So, to Africans:

Leveraging Technology:

"The developed world is moving at a really fast pace, and there is a real gap that exists in almost every aspect between the highly developed and developing countries. However, technology is a wonderful tool and can be used to bridge the gap. Take advantage of it. Learn as much as you can from the latest tools and applications (there's a lot of free information on the Internet, and access to subsidised learning material about almost every subject you can think of.) There is material to download to read; there are webinars, etc. Spend time researching and applying information that adds more value to your life."

Volunteering and Networking:

"Take advantage of opportunities to volunteer or network or work with any organisation or group that does any form of global or international work. This will expose you to working with different cultures and peoples."

Communication and Presentation Skills:

"Seek opportunities to speak and present ideas in small or large groups. This will enhance your ability to gather ideas in a concise manner and to present them effectively to an audience. Learn to communicate well: this includes everything from body language, pitch or tone of voice, to appearance."

Create your value:

"We all have a unique ability inside of us. Find what your unique ability is and operate in it. With some, it is very evident or obvious; with others they are hard to find. Try different things out. Take calculated risks. It is better to take risks when you are younger than when you are older."

Express yourself and be original:

"Find the best way to express yourself, and go do it! This can be through arts and craft, singing, drama, teaching, public speaking, writing (blogging, etc.), playing a sport, dancing, writing software, starting businesses, etc."

If he had to do it all over again, Eric says he would do it differently by starting reading and travelling earlier. He cannot overstate, "How these two activities open up your mind and expose you to so much." I am on the same page with Eric, especially when it comes to travelling, because although I have travelled quite a bit, I wish I had started travelling sooner.

Next on Eric's to-do-list is to try to make a difference wherever he finds himself, by finding ways to inspire and lead others. I think Eric is already on track: his volunteering and participation in the events of various organisations tells volumes. Also, his journey and insights will inspire anyone who reads this book, particularly young Africans.

Louise Rönnerdahl

TO succeed globally, Louise had to exhibit excellent communication and networking skills. She has also been able
to constantly re-invent herself and her thinking in order to
fully understand the global context and the environment she
operates in.

Louise says the one person who influenced her thinking
in a global direction, is her father. He always encouraged her
to discover the world as a way of expanding her thinking
and a way to learn about herself. With such an encouraging
father, Louise could not help, but stay curious about living
abroad and she has done so for most of her professional
life. She has since worked and lived in the United Kingdom,
Germany, Australia, the US, Kenya, Malawi, Rwanda, Sierra
Leone, Côte d'Ivoire, France and Singapore.

From these places, she has learnt a lot about how unique

each country is in the way things work and how people are, and most importantly, the significance of quickly understanding this as a way to integrate successfully. When Louise moved to Kenya, for instance, she spent a month visiting villages and learning people's challenges, life situations and stories, to understand the Kenyan mindset and ways of doing things. Only this way could she then see how she needed to behave to win the trust of the people of Kenya, and respond to their needs. She would have used a completely different approach if she was engaging with another Swedish person for example. Adopting this attitude was critical to her success in Kenya.

Louise studied Business Administration at the University of Stockholm, right in her hometown of Stockholm, which is also the capital of Sweden. But, after working for six years, Louise realised she needed to go back to get an education to refresh her thinking about recent trends and challenges emerging in the world and how to tackle those challenges. To this end, she enrolled on a post-graduate business programme at INSEAD Business School in France.

Although she did not always know what she wanted to do, her parents worked in Finance, so she was naturally influenced to seek the same career path. And with her heart set on Finance at the time, she considered roles offered by the larger accounting firms in Sweden. Louise was very smart about her job search and made sure she built a great network with human resources far in advance of applying for the positions; so once she applied, they already knew who she was.

After a while, she realised she did not find her work fulfilling, and completely changed course and moved to work in education across parts of the African continent.

Louise's past positions include: Accountant at PricewaterhouseCoopers in Stockholm, Sweden; Consultant at PricewaterhouseCoopers in London, United Kingdom; Consultant at Deutsche Bank in London, United Kingdom: Kiva Fellow at Kiva Micro Financing Organisation in Kigali, Rwanda; and Head of Africa Development and Communications at Emerging Leaders in Nairobi, Kenya.

Louise learnt many things from her various roles with these organizations, the most important being the ability to build trusting relationships with other people. She further notes, "If there is no trust, you can't do business. The most important thing in business is to make people want to work with you. There are so many ways of doing this, but having a strong, honest character, showing willingness to work, listen and respect others are very important."

Her last role before the MBA was with the Emerging Leaders NGO in Africa, where she was the Head of Africa Development and Communications. Although she did not apply for this job, she found it through her network in London, where she was working at the time. For this role, she mentions, "I proactively contacted the CEO and offered him my time and skills, for free. He accepted, and after a trial-period of six months where he had been satisfied, he offered me a full-time position." This is truly remarkable and goes to show how driven Louise is.

Having worked for many global organisations, and engaged with people from across the globe on a daily basis.

Louise points out, "The world, with access to new technology, is becoming smaller and smaller and more integrated. Every country is part of a global story, and is affected by what is happening in the rest of the world. It is important for every business person to understand this."

Commenting on some of the skills and attitudes that have given her an edge over others, she candidly points out, "I have a great ability to listen and understand others, and therefore build strong relationships in a global context. I am also very flexible in the way I do business, which I know has been very valuable to my employers. I am also very proactive: instead of sitting around waiting for my boss to give me work, I see problems and try and solve them on my own without having to bother my superiors." Being humble is that one attitude that always does it for her on her global journey. These are really valuable lessons for anyone, especially up-and-coming young graduates from across the globe.

When it came to the skills she had to learn quickly, it was the ability to focus and prioritise what needs to be done, always delivering and communicating effectively, and listening to others. Moving forward, the skill she will like to learn or demonstrate more of, is improving her technical skills, and having a fuller understanding of agriculture.

Some of Louise's challenges of being in a global environment, she says, "There is a lot of uncertainty, as you deal with many stakeholders and they have sometimes conflicting views. How do you influence and make people agree to one course of action, when there is a lack of clear hierarchy and decision-making process? This is very difficult and requires a lot of time, political savvy and patience to resolve." I have no doubt that as determined as Louise is, she will somehow find the balancing act to resolve these uncertainties and conflicts.

If she were hiring a recent graduate, she will search for someone who is very proactive, who can arrive in a new environment and quickly understand what is going on, build relationships with people and get on with things without needing constant supervision.

I asked Louise, to choose graduates from one continent who are about to step out into the world and advice them on what steps to take to succeed globally. Not surprisingly, she chose African graduates and says, "Because I have been working with some of you."

This is Louise's insightful advice: "You are responsible for your own lives. No one is going to come and give you your dream job just like that. You will have to work hard for it. This is the same all over the world, and it can be tough and scary. But, it is possible to create the life you want. You have to be proactive. This means that you need to focus, invest a lot of time and energy to do well at school, and also at building a network of people who work in the industry you are interested in. Try to think in new ways instead of following the beaten path."

She adds that, "The African continent is rising, and there are many opportunities to succeed. Don't sit around and waste time. Time to act is now. Every day you can take a small step in the direction of where you want to go. Remain focused, honest and true and work hard, you will get what you want."

Louise says her greatest career highlight was when she moved from banking in the United Kingdom to Education in Rwanda and realised that she was not confined by one industry, but she had the capabilities to work with many different things, opening doors to even more possibilities in her life.

Will she do anything differently? Louise's response is humbling, considering she made the effort and got out of her comfort zone early; she says "I would have had more courage and belief in myself from the start. This is something I have learnt to nurture over time, and I would have probably been able to go even further if I had the courage from the start."

What is next for Louise? Well, now that she has finished her MBA programme, she says, "we will see! The world is open, ready to be explored."

Bior Bropleh

EVEN though he did not always know what he wanted to do, Bior says, "I just focused on constantly developing myself, and my path led me to where I am today."

Bior initially considered studying Computer Science because he has always been passionate about technological advancement. He also considered International Relations because he appreciated global issues and cultural diversity. Marketing Communications was another area he considered because he had the natural ability to communicate his ideas to gain a following. I worked in the same advertising agency with Bior in Ghana and I have seen his remarkable communications skills and pitching his ideas at play.

He is currently responsible for growing sales with key wholesale accounts for The Home Depot, the world's largest home improvement retailer. His division is a master distributor of plumbing, door hardware and lighting brands.

I wanted to know if getting into his current role was competitive. Bior mentions, "I performed my former role in sales operations very well and transformed the role. It was a challenge but I pushed really hard and had some great achievements. My leadership team appreciated this and offered me more responsibility as a result. It wasn't really competitive."

Bior's track record is very impressive. He is from Monrovia, Liberia, and has worked in 4 other countries. In Ghana, he led AIESEC – the largest student-run organization that facilitates internships all over the world. He later moved to Seoul, South Korea, where he was an organizational development consultant with AIESEC. He returned to Ghana and went straight into the exciting world of Advertising, and managed relationships with some of the biggest brands. He then moved to the US and started off as a sales consultant with AT&T's consumer group. He later moved to The Home Depot and was a case manager in Customer Care before joining their Proprietary Brands group. Finally, he joined the wholesale team primarily managing sales operations for the same company.

Bior shares some key learning points from his past roles. He says, "Roles with AIESEC gave me the worldview and cultural sensitivity to understand various kinds of people. This was invaluable in subsequent Advertising, Marketing and Sales roles. My first sales role in the US gave me a feel of the culture and laid the foundation for other sales roles with AT&T and The Home Depot."

Although he had travelled to the US when he was younger, Bior's first real global encounter happened somewhere very close to home. When he first visited neighbouring Freetown in Sierra Leone, he was mesmerized by how different their culture was from the Liberian culture, but then on some levels it was so similar. His global encounter did not end there as he was further influenced to think in a global direction by both of his parents, who were global citizens who travelled extensively in their careers. His older cousin, Larry Bropleh also influenced him because he had travelled quite a bit and during his AIESEC years, Bior would consult him before he travelled to a new place, because his cousin always had contacts wherever he went.

Bior says he always had a global mindset, because from a very early age, he was fascinated by his parents' travel experiences and loved watching documentaries and shows from different parts of the world. He recalls how in elementary school, he made an effort to speak French with a French accent, even though his classmates made fun of him for that.

To date, Bior has lived in five countries (United States, Sierra Leone, Ghana, South Korea, and Liberia); studied in four countries (United States, Sierra Leone, Ghana, and Liberia); and travelled to roughly 25 countries in Asia, Africa, Europe and North America.

With AIESEC, he travelled for conferences in Africa, Asia, Europe and North America. He found himself on quite a few global teams during that period. In his private

Marketing Consulting, Bior collaborates with contacts from all over the world.

The main lesson he has taken away from these collaborations is, "You have to make sure at the very beginning that all parties are on the same page. With global collaborations, you do not always have the luxury of meeting face-to-face, so it's important that you share similar values. It's always helpful to be mindful of time zone differences as well."

Bior's global outlook is driven by his belief that being and thinking global makes him whole. He says, "It makes me much better, stronger, and more valuable. In every career role, I've utilised this invaluable resource."

Bior believes that to succeed globally, "You just have to be open to new experiences and not judge based on your own upbringing. Always be mindful to take things in context."

Being in a global environment comes with its challenges, and Bior agrees it takes a lot of patience and understanding. He believes one has to get to know and understand other viewpoints and if there is anything you do not understand, you should just let someone know, and eventually you will build trust.

Although he was a bit shy when he was younger, getting along with people from different places was very important for him. This is the one skill he had to learn very quickly.

Regarding the one fallback skill and attitude that works for him every time, he says, "Being personable has really helped me. I have heard from work colleagues that I have the skill of interacting with various groups at various levels."

Bior is planning to acquire a graduate degree soon. He already has an undergraduate degree with double major in

Psychology and Sociology from the University of Ghana. He has received several professional certificates from Kennesaw State University in the US, and he is currently studying for a Project Management Professional certification.

It's not just about certifications for Bior and moving forward: he would like to develop and demonstrate his leadership skills further as he recognises, "The higher you go, the more important it is for you to be able to achieve through others." One of his greatest career highlights is helping to set up a non-profit organisation to help elementary schools in Liberia.

Bior is passionate about the digital revolution and he would want to play a part in using it to change the world. And I know he will, because Bior gets things done.

His advice to graduates the world over is: "Never stop learning!" In his opinion, a global graduate, "Is an individual who has acquired a balanced worldview in their process of studying." If he was hiring a recent graduate, he would look for a person who has similar values. He says, "Skills can be learned, but it's more difficult to get someone with the right mindset."

Sirina Blankson

AS a child, Sirina wanted to be a doctor, and then rightly or wrongly, she wanted to be a pharmacist and follow in her dear old dad's footsteps. But when she moved to the UK after her 1st degree, she considered being a teacher, mainly because it was very easy at the time to find teaching jobs.

At the core, Sirina always knew she was good at the sciences, and when her original plans to study pharmacy did not work out; she opted for Biological Sciences, which she equally loved. With a BSc in Biological Sciences from the Kwame Nkrumah University of Science and Technology in Ghana, and an MSc in Environmental Management from

University of Greenwich in the United Kingdom, all was set
for her to explore and pursue any related career of her choice.

Sirina found her way and has been on an impressive
journey, as her first role was as a Junior Consultant at the
engineering company Mouchel in Manchester UK, where
she was in charge of Environmental Impact Assessments of
infrastructure projects. She then moved on to a Senior Consultant role in Enviros Consulting, undertaking socio-economic impact assessments and environmental impact
assessments in London. Her current role is at the United
Kingdom's National Health Service (NHS) in Kent, as the
Sustainability and Carbon Management Lead.

Sirina mentions that it was very competitive getting into
her current role, because it is a niche industry and the roles
are limited to a specific group of people. It helped that Sirina
had an impressive track record, because when the NHS were
asked to report and cut down on their carbon emissions like
most public sector bodies, she was approached by the organisation in Kent. As she had previously been a Consultant on
Climate Change and Sustainability, the opportunity seemed
like a natural marriage.

Sirina says that her greatest career highlight to date was
when she won an award for the best Carbon Management
Project in the UK in 2011. Sirina has learnt many things
from her past roles. In her very first role, one thing that stuck
with her was that it was always good to be prepared before
you go into meetings. She says, "Sitting there looking pretty
does not cut it: you have to know your stuff. The other thing
I learnt was to always keep it professional as first impressions
do last. This is not a myth."

Sirina's first global encounter was when she project managed a scheme in India in the coal mining industry. She had to communicate with the team in India via teleconference and video links. The concepts of what they were both working towards were the same, but the approach was totally different. In the end, the scheme was a success.

Sirina is a proud Ghanaian who has worked in her home country, the United States of America, and now the United Kingdom. The one thing she has learnt from all these places is tolerance.

The one situation that has influenced Sirina's thinking in a global direction is how most large organisations tend to relegate their corporate responsibilities in Africa mainly because they can get away with it. And she thinks, "It is about time we asked these organisations to pay."

Her global mindset is also being shaped by her desire to acquire knowledge and learn best practices across the globe, and be able to go back home and share these lessons. Networking and sourcing the right interventions to help in Africa is what drives Sirina to be global in her outlook.

As someone who is keen on professional development, she makes sure she attends relevant industry conferences often. Sirina is a member of the International Impact Assessors Association and is currently involved with Women in Environment, a non-profit organisation helping other women in the industry. These industry events, she agrees, facilitate networking and keep one well informed on the highlights of the industry and what's new in terms of legislation.

When I asked Sirina to assess the skills and attitudes she

has brought to the table, she aptly said, "I am very likable and confident. It is good to know and love who you are, which I think I do well. I am firm, and sometimes people expect you to cower under pressure being black and a woman, but it helps to stand tall and firm."

I recall picking up confidence tips from Sirina as a teenager, and it is great to know she has a sense of awareness of this skill and attitude. Tolerance and taking control is an attitude she had to learn quickly. In the future, she would like to learn more about Public Speaking. Hopefully, it will be my turn to return the favour and coach her on this skill.

Sirina is aware of the fact that most graduates tend to take different career paths, and if she were hiring a recent graduate, she would look for someone with the ability to learn. Sirina believes, "Any graduate from any part of the world is a global graduate and the world is your oyster. Be ready to learn, and remember first impressions do last and know your stuff."

Sirina would not do anything differently if she was given the chance. She is equally not rigorously looking out for regrets of missed opportunities in the past, but rather she is looking forward to pass on her knowledge and guide the up-and-coming generation.

Pankaj Goswami

PANKAJ has an MSc in International Hotel Management from the University of Surrey, UK, a Post Graduate Diploma in Management, and a Bachelor of Commerce from Kurukshetra University, India.

When it came to choosing his career path, Pankaj says: "I always wanted to do something in a Finance function, but for me it has not been a straight forward career. When I was looking for my first job, I could not find anything in Finance. The job market was tough and I had increasing pressure to survive, as every year you get an ocean of new graduates. I chose to grab any opportunity I could get, and started my first role in Hotel Operational Management.

Even though I was working in operations, I was very mindful of the company's financial figures, performance and targets. I always made sure that I demonstrated my financial acumen and expressed interest in a finance role as and when the opportunity came. I was fortunate that my Manager recognised my skills and supported a gradual move into the company's Finance Team. I didn't stop after that, and now I'm constantly developing myself to excel in the field."

Pankaj currently works in the Information Technology and Telecommunications industry as the Team Lead for Europe, the Middle East Asian countries (EMEA), with a focus on Financial Planning and Analysis at Verizon Enterprise. His role is perhaps one of the most complex business segments. And to give an idea of the complexities, he says, "I am involved in Financial Planning & Analysis of $2 billion turnover across 20 EMEA countries, over 5,000 customers who buy more than 130 product lines." In his role, he works with a highly competitive team, and it requires taking ownership of not only your tasks, but also the team's performance. As if his role is not challenging enough, Pankaj enrolled on an MBA programme at University of Wales, UK, which he finished in 2014.

Getting into his current role was quite competitive. He applied for the role on Verizon's website and had to go through three rounds of interviews. He thinks the hiring manager was more interested in his Financial knowledge, his communication skills and how he reacted to last minute changes and managed ambiguity and complexity.

Prior to his current role as Team Lead – Financial Planning & Analysis EMEA, Pankaj worked in different positions:

- Food & Beverage Manager – Intercontinental Hotels Group (IHG) – United Kingdom
- Business Analyst – Intercontinental Hotels Group (IHG) – United Kingdom
- Manager – Lidl – United Kingdom
- Management Consultant – HRODC – United Kingdom

When Pankaj traces his steps back to about 11 years ago when he was starting his professional career, he can see he has come a long way and has constantly developed his skills. It did not take him long to realise that communication is the key to success in the professional world. His main focus, whether in the past or present, has always been to improve and update his communication skills to increase social and professional mobility, enhance networking opportunities, share ideas and present his views in an effective way. In addition to communication, he also worked on improving his leadership style to encompass team effort and accountability, and being in a Finance role means Pankaj is constantly learning new techniques of Business Planning and Strategic Management.

Pankaj says: "I think Surrey University was the first 'true' global encounter for me. I am from a very small town in India, so coming to a cosmopolitan and fast paced environment was both exciting and fearful. I used networking as a key to break the gridlock and decided to engage in various group activities and meet people from different backgrounds. That gave a boost to my confidence and helped me in blending into my new environment." Pankaj did 'blend in' well, because I met him while I was also studying at the same university in England.

He was always a breath of fresh air and willing to share his ideas on and off the course. For instance, it was Pankaj who showed me how to really sell myself on a CV so many years ago. I have in turn trained thousands more on how to do so.

Commenting on what influenced his thinking in a global direction, Pankaj says: "I think, for me, it's not people or situations, but rather it's the period I spent in a multi-cultural environment, which has influenced my way of thinking. Over the last decade, I have met many people and been in several situations. Collectively, all of them have given me a unique experience."

Although he has not physically worked in other countries apart from the UK, his current role requires him to work with teams located globally, so it is a virtual work place for Pankaj. He works with teams located in Germany, Belgium, USA, India, Singapore, Hong Kong, Ireland, Australia, the Nordic region, and the Middle East. He has also attended meetings, conferences, seminars and training sessions with colleagues located globally.

When he worked as a Management Consultant, he was involved in coaching Chinese and South Asian delegates for WTO's General Agreement Trades in Services (GATS).

Some of the learning points from these collaborations are:

- Being patient and open to ideas
- Respecting others, their culture and way of thinking

- Communicating in a manner suitable for your audience
- Informal networking always helps you make headway with ideas and views.

Pankaj has so far travelled to Spain, France, Nepal, Morocco and Germany, and every place he visited gave him a different and unique experience – from the people, their culture, their hospitality, their way of interacting, and how they work.

Pankaj says he did not always have a global mindset, because coming from a very small town in India, he had very limited awareness of what was happening around the world. But he says, "I think I was always curious to know new things, which led me to go global. This was the reason I decided to come to UK for higher education. Time spent at University of Surrey helped me explore my own perspective of looking at things and also logically helped the rationalisation of my thinking."

His global outlook is driven by a strong urge to be commercial and politically aware. The desire to move globally with his profession is another driver. And to succeed globally, Pankaj notes that it is important, "to be mindful of the priorities of others and see how they match with yours. Also, understanding different cultures and being open to ideas helps, and most importantly, working on your communication skills and tailoring them according to the environment is critical."

He had to learn quickly, that communication is paramount. Pankaj adds that one has to have the right communication skills to go global. This is because, "Communication is not just about language. It's about expressing one's views in the right manner, attracting others' attention, and pushing through your ideas."

His curiosity and desire to know more has helped him in learning new things, meeting various people and going places. In the future, Pankaj will like to learn and demonstrate more of these skills:

- Communication: Pankaj emphasises on this skill because he believes that there is always room for improvement, and the key is to just keep finding the opportunity to update your skills.
- Curiosity: because for him it is a strange characteristic which helps you find different avenues. He adds, "I love it when my mind keeps questioning me and asks me to go and hunt for the answers."
- Leadership: Working on refining his leadership style to adapt to various cultures.

Personally, Pankaj sees the challenges of being in a global environment as opportunities to learn new things, and he admits that going global has been a learning curve. Over a period of time he has learnt things consciously and sub-consciously, which has equipped him to perform better in today's professional world.

Commenting on the edge he has over others, Pankaj says, "My personal opinion is that everyone has some strengths, and if they keep building on their strengths they can outshine their weaknesses. For me, my curiosity is my strength. I am eager to learn more than the average person, and this keeps me at the forefront of the crowd. It has always helped me to learn new skills and gain a different experience. Perhaps this is the reason I have worked in five different industries (Retail, Banking, Hotels, IT and Consulting), and have performed well in all of them. I have transferrable skills which are tested and applied in different environments to think out of the box and find effective solutions."

Pankaj explains who a global graduate, is in three ways:

Someone who is open to embrace different styles, cultures and viewpoints.

Someone who is eager to learn new things and has a desire to go places

Someone who can communicate effectively and put forward his or her views in an effective manner.

And if he was hiring a recent graduate, these are the attitudes and skills he would look for. The advice and insights he has for any recent or young graduate about to step out into the world are encapsulated in this statement: "One thing I learnt over the years is that professional life is very different from what we study in universities. I would suggest having some sort of practical experience alongside your studies. Also, get engaged in various groups and activities that would enhance your overall personality for teamwork and communication. Be open to ideas and try different things and rationalise your thoughts and acts with logic. You will not succeed all the time, but learning from failure is an art. If you have that, then success is not far."

Pankaj says: "It's a long road and for me: success is not a destination but a journey. I like learning new things and applying them to practice. Professionally, I would like to move to any other global locations to apply what I have learnt to date, and also to give a cutting edge to my career. This would help me stand out in the global market." So far, Pankaj is satisfied with the way things have turned out for him, and instead of analysing the past, he plans for the future.

Sandister Tei

"FIND what you love fast", is Sandister's advice to graduates the world over.

Before age 10, she wanted to be a journalist. Even though she didn't really know what that was, Sandister knew she would always do something related to sharing information.

Having studied for a Bachelor of Arts degree in Geography and Resource Development from the University of Ghana, other career paths such as Medical Geography seemed like a good idea. Sandister thought following disease trends and making the public aware of them, was an interesting concept. Geography generally appealed to her, as information she got from that course helped her filter out a lot of things she heard from the media about Ghana. To this she says, "I just wasn't an ignorant citizen anymore."

Sandister took information related industry internships and extracurricular activities, including copywriting, writing for newspapers and a magazine. She also took a job as an assistant in a pharmaceutical imports company, where she helped set up the company's website, amongst other things.

Sandister trained as a Broadcast Journalist at Cardiff School of Journalism, Media and Cultural Studies (JOMEC), on their International Journalism Master's programme. Sandister currently works for AJ+, Aljazeera's new digital platform. She is also Co-Founder of the Wikimedia Ghana User Group / Lead Editor Retention Program. In addition to this, she acted as the Community Manager at Planning Wikimedia Ghana, an organisation she co-founded through the support of Wikimedia Foundation, the parent organisation for Wikipedia.

Sandister points out that her undergraduate degree at the University of Ghana hugely prepared her for the academic life in Cardiff. Although her past work experiences did not prepare her directly for her current broadcast training, as she did not have a background in radio and TV journalism, character-wise, the general work ethics learnt in her past helped her recognise the need to conduct herself professionally. What she learnt most in Wales when she was studying, was that quality education is highly likely to yield quality minds.

Sandister says her first ever-global encounter started from 'my mother's living room, watching so much foreign

TV'. In primary school, she was among some of the kids who always got chosen to interact with internationals who visited the school. She says, "I had an awareness that Ghana wasn't alone on this planet. There were others who are different from us, so I was open to interactions."

Commenting on the one person, thing or situation that has influenced her thinking in a global direction, Sandister says "I attended an event by the career consultancy SPEC Consult. I later became an intern there. The Principal Consultant (Edem Adzaho, the author of this book) had experienced both Ghanaian and international career and academic cultures. She gave me a lot of books and advice on how to think globally for my education and career. The Internet also shaped me."

The Internet indeed did shape Sandister, because for a while, she was a Social Media Consultant, who also leveraged her curiosity and skills and taught herself html, and designed several websites for several businesses, including my company website (www.specconsult.com). Though she is based in Ghana, Sandister has since worked for businesses with international branches.

She believes Ghana will always come first. But, when she needs to deliver for a global audience, she should be capable of doing so with no restrictions. Sandister's work with Planning Wikimedia Ghana has taken her to Hong Kong and London for conferences for all Wikimedians across the globe. A job with AJ+, has taken her to the USA as well as gets her to interact with colleagues from all over the world.

When it comes to the key learning from such global collaborations, Sandister is of the strong view that "The world needs solutions. I have become solution-oriented in a lot of things I do now. If it doesn't answer a question, I don't do it." The one skill Sandister brings to the table every time is being self-aware as she thinks, "If you don't know who you are, you are a hazard unto yourself." Having a storytelling strength, which is required for Journalism, is the one skill she would like to learn and demonstrate more of in the future.

Sandister's challenge in a global environment is "Being exposed to cultures which are not exposed to you or yours," and "You could get easily outraged", she adds. Knowing Ghana has global neighbours who are different, drives her own global mindset.

Career-wise and academically, her output is not just measured against just Ghanaians, but there are Nigerians, Chinese, Americans, British, South Africans and so on. Even if she was in a local context, she likes world-class output. To Sandister, a global graduate is "One that can fit anywhere globally in their industry." As a start-up owner, if she were hiring a recent graduate, she would look for "A graduate who is willing to learn and has an interest in the industry, not one just looking for a job."

If she had to do it all over again, would she do it differently? She confesses, "I wish I had gone into broadcasting right after my BA. I would have had more hours in the industry." We can only watch out for this young and driven woman, whose global career is starting off. Sandister is ready for the world and the world is no doubt ready for her.

Dr Laila Kassam

LAILA says, "A global graduate is someone with no physical barriers." Born in England to parents from Tanzania with Indian heritage, it looks like Laila was set on her global journey from birth. Laila's regular email updates to me are never boring. They breathe with enthusiasm, drive and purpose. Over the course of a few months, she is in Ghana for work; then in Malawi with people from all over the world to learn how to build an Earthship; then she goes to Guatemala to learn about permaculture; travels to Canada to take time out to see family, and then goes back to London to defend her PhD thesis.

She has just come back from northern Mozambique where she is working with an international NGO to develop a strategy for the development of a 'green school', to teach secondary school students in rural areas about sustainability. She is off next to St. Lucia to design a project with a local NGO on sustainable living through demonstrating natural building methods and sustainable agriculture.

Laila is a freelance Development Economist who has an MSc from London School of Economics, and a PhD from SOAS, University of London. Her thesis topic: "Assessing the contribution of aquaculture to poverty reduction in Ghana," proves her passion for development. She always knew she wanted to work in international development and was willing to work hard and for no money in order to get relevant experience and exposure. This move was quite strategic, and she knew she was paying her dues and was confident that at the right time, she would be recommended for future opportunities, which is exactly what happened.

As someone who has always been open to opportunities, Laila went to India to volunteer for a period during her first degree. Her first real job was with the high profile Aga Khan Foundation. She wanted to volunteer for the Foundation, but instead they offered her a job in Geneva. Laila later worked on the Foundation's other projects in Kenya and the Kyrgyz Republic. She spent a year in Kenya assessing the poverty impact of one of the Foundation's rural development projects in Coast province. Her time in Kenya, she says, "Was a real baptism of fire". She had to work with a tiny budget to survey 900 rural households in the project area. Her experience in Kenya revealed how resilient, flexible and adaptable she could be. She learnt how to function in sometimes dysfunctional environments, and as a result, always found new and different ways to do things.

She has also worked in Guyana as an Overseas Development Institute (ODI) Fellow for the Ministry of Agriculture; undertaken consultancies for the World Fish Centre in Malaysia; and the Food and Agriculture Organisation (FAO) of the United Nations, in Rome, with whom she has travelled to India, Thailand, Ghana, Uganda and Zambia, for short term assignments.

With all these experiences, no wonder she is able to work with different people from different backgrounds. Laila strongly believes, "One needs to be open minded to be able to live abroad." Laila has always believed she can learn and do anything. To this end, she is determined to build an off-the-grid, natural, sustainable eco-lodge in Ghana. I have actually lost count of the number of times she has been to Ghana. She's a very focussed and inspiring individual. Ghana will be blessed to have her.

Although Laila has relatives in Canada and has travelled a lot as a child on trips from London to Rome, it was actually her father who really influenced her thinking in a global direction. Her father, who also works in international development, always travelled abroad for work and would send postcards from exotic places, and these got her really excited about seeing the world.

Her first real global encounter was going to visit relatives in Gujarat India when she was 14 years old. She got a culture shock when she came face to face with extreme poverty in the slums of Bombay. Laila says: "I was so upset by that experience: the shock stayed with me and ultimately influenced my career choice."

Laila associates her global success to a combination of attitudes, skills and other factors, like luck and opportunity. She emphasises that one always has to be prepared for opportunity. For instance, although she loved Kenya and had given her best at the job, she was recommended to apply for the ODI Fellowship and ended up working in Guyana, South America, where she had another great experience.

Laila believes that being at the right place at the right time, having a goal and believing that you are going to get there, is important. Also, having a positive 'can do' attitude and good interpersonal skills are crucial, she says. For instance Laila is able to work with both farmers and directors in the same breath.

Laila mentions that humility is important because she believes everyone is there to teach you something. She hopes to develop her leadership skills further, as well as find more creative solutions to the various challenges in her field. Laila's own personal challenge as a global graduate is how her life has evolved, and this has resulted in having a worldview and perspective that is very different from some of her friends. She also mentions that it can be difficult to keep moving and not settle down, though she feels the trade-off is worth it right now, as every day is different and exciting.

Working in the field, she says, "Can be challenging and rewarding in many ways."

With the kind of work she does, Laila had to quickly learn new skills like quantitative skills, undertaking surveys, and flexibility. Next for Laila, is to have her development consultancy business up and running and move to Ghana to set up her revolutionary eco-lodge and permaculture farm, a social enterprise through which she can engage in grassroots community development.

Laila recalls working with National Service personnel in Kumasi, Ghana, who were ambitious and saw their National Service as an opportunity to learn. Her advice to graduates is "To be positive and make the best of every opportunity. Work out what you want to do and do it well, not just for the money. If you do what you love, the money will follow."

Sydney Hushie

SYDNEY is a Ghanaian who studied Economics at Central University College in Ghana. Though Sydney has lived in Ghana all his life, his work cuts across all the continents, and this has exposed him to the many global challenges we face, and how common they are across borders.

Sydney studied science in high school, because like most of his peers growing up, he wanted to be a pilot. After a while, though, he switched to wanting to be a doctor. He says, "When I found myself leading the school debate team and leading the Students' Council as a senior prefect, I realised that what I really wanted to do was to be an advocate. This was something that came to me easily."

Most of us dreamt and wished to be in certain careers, only to find out we either did not have the aptitude for it or we were not willing to stretch ourselves far enough to pursue it. The list of broken, unfulfilled dreams laced with excuses are endless, and this clearly does not apply to Sydney.

Sydney started his career quite early, and not everyone can say that. His career choice came about as a result of his interest in speaking for others as early as nine years old. He found himself defending his friends on many occasions. He then joined a children's media advocacy group at Ghana Broadcasting Corporation, to put the passion to good use while shaping it for collective good.

Sydney's first global encounter was at age 15, when he represented Ghana at the 4th World Summit on Media for Children in Thessaloniki in Greece, where he was to contribute to developing a global guideline for involving children in the media.

In a country where most people assume they need university qualifications before they even apply for jobs or go on an internship, Sydney applied for his first job with an international advocacy group based in the USA when he had not even started his university studies. He got the job after a number of interviews, largely through experience and demonstration of will and his ability to deliver.

Sydney's passion really knows no bounds, as he currently has two major high profile jobs: he works as a Youth Development Consultant with the British Council, and he also does international advocacy for the rights of young people, on various development indicators including employment, reproductive health and human rights. This means he works with and for the African Union, the United Nations and other development agencies on these issues.

Sydney has worked as a programmes coordinator managing 12 staff across Africa and leading development projects in Asia, South America and Africa. His work with the British Council has spanned over five years, leading to a number of sustainable projects. Currently, he is responsible for new initiatives and partnerships.

I have been lucky to work on at least two of Sydney's projects at the British Council, and to say that he is remarkable and extraordinary will be a huge understatement.

Sydney's past roles have been very practical. They have demanded a lot of research and partnerships. He had to learn writing and developing concepts and initiatives. This has prepared him for his current roles, which involve a lot of market intelligence gathering and concept development.

Sydney's global thinking is inspired by the numerous challenges we face as a people. He says, "I am not the kind who would sit around and wait for others to get the work done. So long as we have challenges, which cut across borders, I see myself motivated to keep looking at seeking global solutions to solve local challenges."

His global mindset has been shaped along the way, because when he started working with young people, he was motivated by the need to create change or contribute to creating change. He did not see where it would take him. It just happened to have taken an international dimension. However, his focus is always to maintain relevance in his country and to the grassroots where the marginalised are in the majority.

Sydney has been involved in a number of global collaborations. He has been involved in developing a number of the youth initiatives by the African Union including the Youth Volunteer corps that sends skilled African youth across the continent to contribute to development. He has been a major player in the post 2015 discussions of the Millennium Development Goals. Sydney has also conducted various training sessions for young people across the world, and raised over one million dollars in grants to support development projects by young people across the world.

These collaborations, he says have honed his skills in partnerships and social mobilisation of young people. To work and succeed globally, Sydney agrees that it involves appreciating diversity and thinking beyond your local situation. It also involves building cross border partnerships to develop global solutions. And for him, largely appreciating diversity and the difference in knowledge has been an asset.

Sydney points out the many challenges of being in a global environment. Among them are:

- The level of intolerance for different views by current leaders
- Adapting to the local context everything that is developed at the global level
- The challenge of securing local support for global initiatives
- His personal challenges have been the constant changing of the development landscape, which demands a constant upgrade and a refresher of skills

The one skill he had to learn quickly was writing. This is because a lot of the writing he did over the years was for sensational stories. He had to adapt this skill to developing concepts and proposals. Moving forward, diplomacy is the one skill he is hoping to shape a lot. This is due to the level of frustration he feels about the growing apathy towards how long it takes for change to happen.

If he were hiring a recent graduate, Sydney says, "I would look for an individual who can apply him or herself in different contexts and demonstrate a will to support global development. I would look at someone who has an open mind and appreciates diversity. A global graduate would understand his or her local context and apply it to providing solutions that cuts across borders."

His advice to recent graduates or any one about to step out into the world is, "Primarily, there are many problems in the world to make anyone relevant in the global space. You need to understand what your skills are, what you are passionate about and get started."

If he had to do it all over again, Sydney says: "I would spend a lot of time concentrating on specifics rather than spreading thinly across different issues." The plan now is to run into Law School to take the advocacy a step higher. I personally feel the world is ready for the likes of Sydney.

Nicole Maske

NICOLE always had a global mindset. She has always been interested in learning about different countries and has always seen herself as part of a global community – able to travel and interact with people from all over the world. It comes as no surprise that Nicole has been selected by the World Economic Forum as a Global Shaper for her country Namibia.

Apart from studying in South Africa and the UK, she has worked in Namibia, South Africa and Nigeria. Nicole has also travelled extensively to Kenya, Zimbabwe, Botswana, Mozambique, Germany, Maldives, Guatemala, Mexico, Belize, USA, Iceland, France, Malta, Austria, Switzerland, Romania, Luxembourg, Spain and Italy.

Nicole has learnt a lot from all these places: mostly that "People are different, we have different realities, and it is important to respect each other and these differences." Looking back, Nicole says going to London as a teenager was her first global encounter. She recalls, "Things were very different from Namibia: the buildings were much older, the weather was terrible, the roads were different, there were more people and different brands. I had been to South Africa, Botswana and Zimbabwe before that, but London was completely different."

Nicole has a Bachelor of Business Science in Actuarial Science from University of Cape Town; she is a Fellow of the Actuarial Society of South Africa and has an MBA from London Business School. Her London Business School experience was a very good global collaboration, because she believes different realities and cultures shape the way we see the world and the way we do business. Her global outlook is driven by an interest in other people, cultures and countries, and a need to feel part of a bigger global community.

Although, she did not always know what she wanted to do, and is not sure that she does now, as a Global Shaper, I am confident Nicole is shaping mindsets and impacting her generation in many ways. Some of the possible career paths she considered were: Healthcare Actuary in an actuarial consulting firm, Consulting Actuary, Equity Analyst or investment management. Nicole has since worked as a Business Analyst at McKinsey and Company and as an Actuarial Strategy Consultant for Liberty, both in Johannesburg. Some of the things Nicole learnt from these past roles that has prepared her for the future are:

- Ability to interact with senior people comfortably and effectively
- Excellent communication, both written and verbal
- PowerPoint skills – putting together the story, doing the slides, and ensuring the message comes across well
- How to deal with difficult people and influence people
- How to assimilate large quantities of information

Nicole is currently a Business Development Manager for Old Mutual Namibia, and an Executive Business Assistant to the MD of Old Mutual Africa. On getting her current role, it might have been the case of having an impressive track record, being proactive, as well as being at the right place at the right time. She recounts, "I visited Namibia in the summer break of my MBA, to meet people and understand the pros and cons of moving back, as well as the career opportunities. I met with an actuary at Old Mutual for coffee and gave her my CV in case she heard of an interesting role for me. She passed it on to the CEO of Old Mutual Namibia, who immediately recognised the match with the Executive Business Assistant position they were trying to fill. I met with the MD in London to discuss the role and he explained that they wanted to broaden the role to include the Business Development scope."

To succeed globally, Nicole observes, "You need to be respectful of different people and cultures, with their different way of doing things and seeing the world. You need to be able to adapt to different environments: ensure that you behave, communicate, dress, etc. appropriately for that situation."

To have an edge over others, Nicole has deployed her ability to communicate clearly, in a structured way; she has a sense of maturity for her age; and the capacity to interact comfortably with her seniors. She is highly motivated and driven, with a hardworking attitude. The one skill she relies on every time, is her communication ability.

Nicole also had to quickly learn to have a positive attitude by, "Looking for ways to make something happen rather than looking for reasons why it will not work." Above all, Nicole has also learnt to "not sweat the small stuff," choosing her battles, because we all see things differently. Moving forward, she would like to demonstrate more of her positivity.

Some of the challenges she sees as a result of being in a global environment are: much more competition with many highly skilled global people, trying to keep up with everything that is going on, and working with people who have a different outlook and different ways of working.

A global graduate, she says, "Is someone who has worked or lived in different countries and shows evidence of being culturally agile" and if she were hiring a recent graduate, these are some of the things she will look for. Nicole regrets nothing in her life and will not change or do anything differently. Her advice is aimed more at African graduates: "Go and live abroad somewhere. Gain experience, insights and skills which you can bring back to your home country to make a difference and be successful."

What is next for Nicole? She says, "Only time will tell."

Charles Odoom

CHARLES has a Bachelor's degree in Finance and Accounting from the University of Ghana Business School, and an MBA from Nyenrode Business Universiteit, Netherlands. His MBA programme also took him to China and the USA.

Although he did not have a specific career path in mind, Charles wanted to acquire a professional discipline to run his future business. Running his own business is still on the list, but for now Charles is with Pricewaterhouse-Coopers (Ghana) Ltd. and is in Strategy and Operations Consulting.

His past roles have been as a Financial Accountant for Nestlé Central and West Africa, Free Zones Compliance Coordinator on Legal and Tax for Nestlé Central and West Africa and a Pre-shipment Inspections Officer for Gateway Services Limited.

Charles mentions that a good understanding of organisational systems and operations, financial analysis, reporting, compliance and risk management, are some of the things he learnt from his past roles. These skills have ultimately prepared him for this current one in Strategy and Operations Consulting with PricewaterhouseCoopers, a role he applied for after Business School.

Charles's passion for Geo-Politics and Global Socio-Political and Economic conspiracy theories is what has influenced his thinking in a global direction. His first global encounter was at a youth conference of the World Bank in Accra. This conference shaped his global mindset, and now he has acceptance and tolerance for all, whether African or Non-African.

Charles is a native of Ghana and has worked in at least three different countries. He has lived, studied or travelled to a number of countries across the continents, including, but not limited to South Africa, Egypt, Zimbabwe, Nigeria, The Netherlands, UK, Belgium, France, Germany, Italy, Poland, Russia, USA and China.

The key lessons from all these places are, "There is always some good somewhere in the world, and we are just one people." The global collaborations he has been involved in are: His Graduate (MBA) education; AIESEC conferences and meetings as a result of being a member of AIESEC;

youth and other global conferences; child rights advocacy and activism engagements; global CSR initiatives; and professional and social online communities and groups. Charles says he appreciates the importance of synergy, building relationships, networks and the vast opportunities for further global professional collaborations.

For Charles, it is a matter of necessity and trend that drives his global outlook.

Open-mindedness, being able to build and manage global relationships and networks, as well as trustworthiness and professionalism, have been the ingredients he has used to succeed globally. Having a positive outlook on life has been crucial too.

Charles is aware that being consistently competitive is a key challenge in a global environment, and the edge he has over others professionally, is his "superior training and attitude to execute his engagements." He also has a network of friends who are professionals from all over the world, whom he can count on to deliver superior quality and value to his clients, if he ever needed them to.

For someone who works in Finance, personal financial management in hard times was a skill he had to learn fast. And the one skill he would like to learn or demonstrate more of is patience. Charles says if he had the chance to do anything differently, he will do it exactly the same way, "Because the present is always too harsh on history and I do not want to fall into that trap."

For him, a global graduate is someone who demonstrates a willingness to challenge the status quo and is open-minded enough to reach beyond his or her environs for solutions that can stand the test of time. His advice to all graduates aspiring to be global is, "There is no limit to one's potential. You may not achieve all your dreams, but do your best not to regret for never trying."

Milena Conolly

With Milena in Brussels

WHEN it came to the possible career paths Milena considered, she says, "I thought about acting or something in the arts, but my parents always told me that I could never make money or a career in these areas. They viewed these activities as extracurricular and encouraged me to view them as such. I never did agree with this thinking, but I was taught that you followed your parent's advice whether you agreed or not."

Food Server, Restaurant Supervisor, Office Assistant, Office Manager, Director of the Tourism Association,

Accounts Assistant, Manager of the Credit Card Department, Cancer Registrar are a cocktail of roles Milena has had over the years.

Although she says she still has no idea what she wants to do, she knows what she enjoys and tries to work with these, wherever she is employed. Milena's focus is on doing something that meets her personal beliefs.

For someone who has tried out a number of roles and has been blessed with quite a few career highs like landing great positions and being promoted quickly into the highest positions at times, one wonders which she will consider as a career highlight. Most surprisingly, she says, "It has been the career lows that have had the greatest impact. The realisation that family, time, sticking to my morals and beliefs were more important than labels, titles and money have all come about from career lows and are therefore the highlights of my career."

Before university, Milena realised how much she loved her Islands and could easily share this love with others by working in the service industry. Her aim then was on becoming as highly trained as possible, so as to contribute to making the Cayman Islands Tourism product one of the best in the World. Milena then decided to go to the best and learn how she could better promote her country. She chose the University of Surrey in the South of England, which has consistently been ranked number one in the UK for hospitality and tourism programmes, by The Guardian, The Times and The National Student Survey for both her undergraduate and postgraduate degrees. It is not surprising that in 2015, The University of Surrey ranked 4th overall in the 2016 The Guardian league table after Oxford, Cambridge and St Andrews.

Milena had her BSc in International Hospitality and Tourism Management, followed by an MSc in eTourism.

At University, Milena recalls taking some law courses as part of her undergraduate programme, which she thoroughly enjoyed, but she was not ready to commit to the years of studies required to follow this career path. Surrey felt just like home, hence her decision to pursue her postgraduate study there as well. She says she loved the diversity of the community at the University.

Unfortunately, the fear of technology and change she encountered became very frustrating when she returned home. This is an experience I can personally relate to as I was on the same eTourism course with Milena at Surrey and had a similar experience when I relocated home.

At Surrey, Milena also found she enjoyed accounting, but never had an aptitude for such studies. Although she is not a qualified accountant, she enjoys working in accounts and is currently working in the Accounts division of the Cayman Islands Judicial Department, where she works on several different projects from updating interest on accounts to developing the credit card payment system. She says, "My role is very diverse: at times I am a cashier whilst other times I am in the back office arranging bill payments."

With such an impressive and versatile track, I wondered if it was competitive for Milena to get into her current role, and she mentions that an ex-co-worker recommended her to her current boss. She went to drop off her CV, did the job test on the spot and was interviewed. That was a Friday, and by Monday afternoon, she had a signed contract and was working.

She has no idea how many other candidates there were, but she is aware of the unemployment problem on the island and how at the moment qualified individuals are without work for 6 to 12 months. Milena did find out later why she got the job: All the jobs she did connected all the dots. Her employer mentioned there were quite a few things about her CV that made her eager to hire her. Milena says, "My past experience with credit cards, project management and the software I had used in previous jobs met the needs they had for the role. They initially thought they wouldn't be able to find someone with all the skills they needed and had opted to find a more junior person so they could train and enlist current staff to take on bits and pieces of the projects."

There are three main things Milena has learnt from her past roles that prepared her for her current one. These are:

"Money isn't everything – As the company can't pay the usual salary she would expect, they have offered her the most pay they can and less hours. There have been past roles that paid much better but certainly didn't give her the time she wanted and didn't make her as happy. With this role, she no longer dreads Monday mornings."

"You can learn from everyone around you – The pride and details she has seen from some previous co-workers and the laziness and dishonesty of some were great life lessons. She can now look at each staff member, and see how his or her work affects the entire process. This will help her in developing a system that will work for everyone."

"The need to stick to your morals and set your own standard of work". Milena had some difficult situations in her past roles. Some situations came about where she was encouraged to lie or was presented with lies. No job is worth giving up your morals for. She now works with sensitive information relating to the courts and can feel comfortable and confident in her own ethics.

Milena's first global encounter happened on the nearby island of Jamaica. She says of the time: "A classmate and I were selected by the Rotary Club to go on an exchange to Jamaica which is only an hour's flight away. We stayed with a prominent Chinese Jamaican family who owned a sweet factory that distributed globally. I had never considered the diversity of the Caribbean and how global our communities and businesses were until then."

The experience in Jamaica definitely influenced her thinking in a global direction, and the Scottish teacher who helped arrange the trip was also a good influence. He taught her Math, (her worst subject), but he never acted as though her family's financial circumstance or her lack of comprehension in his class limited her. She says, "At that time, if you weren't "smart" you weren't exposed to many opportunities to leave the island. I wanted to explore; see and do more. So, when the Rotary Club offered another exchange opportunity I jumped at it. I was sent to Turkey for a year and that experience really helped shape my thinking and view of the world. I am not sure you can get more global than a Caribbean person in the Middle East."

Milena was born in Belize, as were her parents. Her grandfather on her father's side was from the Cayman

Islands. Her mother, being an adventurer in her own right, found a job in the Cayman Islands and moved permanently when Milena was two years old. In Milena's heart and mind she is equally from Belize and the Cayman Islands.

She has worked in the Cayman Islands and England. And although she has only worked in two countries, most of her work has given her the opportunity to work with others in different countries, as most of her employers had connections in other countries. For example, much of her work with Philips Electronics in England required her to communicate with colleagues in Poland on a daily basis and from time to time, with organisations in India. Her work with the Cayman Cancer Registry gave her the opportunity to work with other registries and health institutions in the Caribbean and North America. In Banking, she was also given the opportunity to work with others in the Bahamas, USA and Panama.

Milena's footprint is dotted across pretty much all the continents:

- Central America - Belize, Mexico and Panama.
- North America - USA (including Alaska) and Canada.
- South America - The Colombian islands of Providence and San Andres, Ecuador, Peru and Guyana.
- Africa – Kenya.
- Europe - England (studied & lived there), Scotland, Spain, the Canary Islands, Belgium, Turkey (studied & lived there), Italy, Amsterdam, Norway, Sweden, Finland.
- Asia - Bali, Australia.

- Caribbean - Cayman Islands (studied & lived there), Jamaica, Cuba, Puerto Rico, US Virgin Islands, Trinidad, the Bahamas, and St. Martin.

In each one of these places, she had the opportunity to learn about other people, the places, her work, and about herself.

Her global collaborations cut across various sectors:

- Banking: Bahamas head office, Panama for outsourced services, and Miami for training.
- Tourism: Conferences in Puerto Rico and mainland USA.
- Accounting: Offices in Poland, outsourced services in India.
- Cancer Registry: other Caribbean registries, USA organisations and research centres, conferences in Canada, and training in the Caribbean and the USA.

She learnt so much from these collaborations – particularly on negotiations and networking. The key learning points for her were:

She learnt a lot about presentations and how important it is to get your information across so that others understand and get on board with your ideas. She thinks, "It is one of the first steps in getting the connections you need to become global."

Understanding others' needs and showing them how you can fulfil those needs or assist them in achieving their goals, was another learning point. Milena points out, "This will encourage others to work with you no matter where in the world you are, how small your business is or how limited your services are."

It is no surprise, that Milena has always had a global mindset. She says, "Growing up in Cayman we were always exposed to the history of our men being seamen and establishing homes, families and businesses in many countries. My name was found on one of my father's trips to Italy. My Belizean heritage also featured a mixing of global minded individuals. My Great grandparents were a mix of indigenous Maya Indian, Spanish, British and a Mestizo, all of whom were globally minded and ventured away from their local environments to explore and seek new opportunities. My mother also brought us up with an appreciation for other cultures and a desire to see it and experience it all."

Milena also points out that the knowledge and experiences of others are very alluring, and these drive her to have a global outlook. One wonders if Milena has missed any opportunities as a result of not being strategically global in her outlook. She says, "I don't believe so. I try to live by the ideas of taking advantage of every opportunity" and if it didn't happen, it wasn't the right time. There have been times, though, where I think the lack of global thinking has affected and limited the organisations I have worked with. This was very frustrating to bear witness and sometimes to be involved with. It is probable that the most difficult thing to see is someone or a business limiting their development because they are not thinking globally."

To succeed globally, Milena advocates for the acceptance of habits and cultures of who and what people are.

Understanding the needs of the end users of a process or product is important too. And in her personal experience, by being open to experiences and being ready to learn from others, she has been able to succeed globally.

Apart from adopting the attitude of accepting each person for who and where they are, Milena points out that being ready to learn from others, whether their jobs be big or small; taking time to understand them and their role in the entire process, allows her to see the big picture like a puzzle. This is because each little piece is important and contributes to making the puzzle whole. Also, being open to change has always given Milena an edge over others. Many people are afraid to think and do things differently, she adds.

In spite of all these, Milena had to quickly learn that it is important to trust your instincts in the work place. She adds, "Your colleagues don't have to be friends, and not everyone who smiles is really happy." Above all, she learnt that it is more important to listen rather than talk, because you will learn a lot that way. She strongly believes, "The things you hear can help you succeed."

Moving forward, Milena would like to demonstrate more confidence in the skills she has, and also have patience with people's inability to change and think globally. In her global journey, Milena has found communication - the languages, tones and body language, and knowledge of the customs, phrases, religions and political situations, to be challenging.

Now then, who does Milena think is a global gradu-ate? She says, "I have met many, but the top – my mother, Edem (the author of this book), Ewelina and Sezen (Sezen has also been profiled for this book). I point out these people because they have been examples to many. They have shown that no matter where we come from, and what path we take, it is possible to see, accept and adapt to the global elements of life in business and personally." And if she were hiring a recent graduate, Milena would hire someone with honesty, integrity, determination, eagerness to learn and solutions driven.

Milena's advice for any graduate is, "Remember that not everyone lives and thinks and has access to the same things as you. Don't make assumptions that because they don't, that they are any less than you or you can't learn from them. Know that as an individual, what makes you different are the life experiences that make you most valuable to any organisation. Embrace who you are and offer that in your work each day."

Millena says she will not do anything differently if she was to do it all over again, and only God knows what is next for her. What she does know is, she looks forward to it. And all she can do in preparation is to enjoy and learn as much as she can, in the present.

Yaw Mante

TO succeed globally, Yaw agrees that the underlying values are the same everywhere. Hard work and grit are important and if you want to work in an increasingly global world, curiosity is also important. Having the confidence and willingness to question things that don't make sense also counts.

Yaw is from Ghana and grew up there. He has worked briefly in the US and mostly in the UK, and has travelled to a number of countries in Europe. He attended Yale University and studied Economics for his undergraduate degree, where his senior project focused on the impact of mobile phone technology on economies in Sub-Saharan Africa. He has also completed the CFA, a professional program focused on Investment Management. He says he did it for its focus on equity valuation.

Even though he was not set on one specific job, one thing he was sure of was to have a broad experience early in his career. Yaw felt his way around and discovered interesting aspects of what he wanted to do along the way.

Some of the possible career paths he considered included Consulting, Banking, and Entrepreneurship.

He currently does M&A (mergers & acquisition) execution as part of an advisory team within Barclays' cards and payments business. Getting into his current role was competitive, because although he had moved from another area within the wider firm, he points out that generally, Corporate Finance roles are competitive. He went through the standard interview process: four rounds of interviews: a key part was the technical interview that reviewed candidates' grasp of finance theory and financial valuation. There was also a 'fit' interview to access how you carried yourself and how well you would fit into the team.

Yaw's greatest career highlight was when he advised one of the internal teams on one of the largest real estate outsourcing deals in the UK's financial services sector. His first job was in M&A at Lehman Brothers, where he advised clients in European technology and industrial space. He then did a short stint with a Ghanaian start-up, where he was mostly responsible for marketing, general strategy and oversight. Then he moved to Barclays where he did some internal consulting (market research, strategy, analytics) within operations at the Bank.

Some of the things Yaw learnt from his past roles that have prepared him for his current role are:

- Modelling and comfort in Excel is critical in his current role. His analytics experience really improved his data manipulation skills.
- His experience running a number of projects with people from different departments, was useful Project Management training.
- The need to sometimes keep challenging your manager to support your professional growth, as one has to be very clear and explicit about what his or her aims are. And if you want a promotion within a time frame, then you have to talk to the manager about it: ask them whether it is doable and ask them to support you and guide you through the process."
- Do not lose sight of what your career goals are. "You should keep discussing with your team lead how the projects you support and the tasks you do would help you grow."

Yaw has been involved in a number of collaborations in a volunteering capacity and in his professional life. One such project he highlights is working with one of the operations teams to upgrade their cost management principles: as a result, he ended up training the procurement leads across 11 or so countries at a conference. The key learning point he gained from such collaborations is, "There are differences between cultures that are not obvious before you start inter-acting with people from across those different cultures or countries. Being aware of this is the key lesson." He points out that once you become aware of the subtleties, you may use it as you see fit, depending on the context.

When it comes to the skills he had had to learn quickly, Yaw had to learn a lot of Excel modelling skills very quickly in the beginning of his working life. Other areas, he says takes time. For example, learning to be a good team lead actually requires lots of practice.

Yaw says it is difficult to choose one skill that does it for him every time, but he would go for the one that facilitates the use of all the other skills; because in his working life, he has learnt the most when he faced projects that in the beginning, he had no idea how to do or complete. What has always taken him from that stage to a completed and suc-cessful project is the belief that the problem can be solved: it can be cracked, and he has the ability and the resources to see the task to conclusion. This, to him is the first step before all the other skills are actually employed to solve the problem.

His competitive edge has been to try to cultivate the ability to work equally effectively across numbers, abstract concepts and purely creative challenges. The goal for him is to see more of the different aspects of complex problems, which makes for more effective problem solving.

Yaw's global outlook is driven by part interest, part necessity. He says, "The world of work is increasingly becoming global in outlook, and the workplace is becoming more diverse. I can work better if my awareness of the world is better. Plus there is so much richness in the wider world to explore: whatever your interests: food, art, books, stories, music, etc."

He recalls his first global encounter as, "Reading as a kid, about English history, Chinese fables (the Magic Deer, Monkey King), and Japanese traditional arts. I read my Dad's encyclopaedia set and this really amazing book of activities from around the world—it had all the party games you could think of, and it also had tips on stuff like bird watching. These books opened up other parts of the world to me. I also remember interactions with family members who lived outside Ghana. But, by far the most immersive experience was when I went to University in the US."

Wondering what influences Yaw's thinking in a global direction, he says, "It was a gradual confluence of experiences during my university years in the US. There was no one moment. I realised that being an international student or an expat, I was forced to think globally. You could not help judging values, standards and attitudes in your host environment by those you were more comfortable with. With this experience, you noticed that no culture or environment had the best way of doing everything."

His thinking has evolved over time, and he is much more aware of the world. He also has a better understanding of the histories of parts of the world, and he appreciates cultural differences more. A lot of the values he grew up with came from Ghana. He says a lot of those values were questioned, discussed, thought about and modified in those formative university years in the US, though his references in working life came from the UK. He learnt that better teams were made up of people from diverse backgrounds, and he appreciates the fact that diversity in views, when harnessed well, can be very useful.

For him, the challenge of being in a global environment is that diverse teams can be difficult to negotiate if not managed well. Yaw also feels if he spoke two or three more languages (perhaps another European language, Chinese, or Swahili), his world would open up so much more and will equally mean more opportunities – professional and personal – would be within reach. I feel the same, as all the neighbouring countries of Ghana are French speaking, but I can only get by with minimal conversational French. And although I speak about 7 other Ghanaian languages, 2 of which can help me make conversations in parts of Nigeria, Togo and Benin, I would have really loved to speak more international languages, especially French: something I am working on.

However, Yaw needs not worry too much about this, as he is a great abstract artist and his work will transcend many languages across the globe. For someone aiming at targeted professional growth, he would also like to focus more on the softer side: things like building and managing relationships, business development, managing teams better, improving his presentation skills, as well as thinking more about leadership. If he had to do it all over again, he would gain his broad experience, which he really values, in a much shorter time, if possible.

When it comes to who Yaw thinks is a global graduate, he says, "This question cuts to the heart of what the word 'global' means. For me, being global denotes an awareness and curiosity about the world beyond your immediate environment. Being global also means you understand that no one system, country or culture has the best answers to all problems. And finally, the global mind has a certain tolerance and perhaps celebration of the diversity in values and worldviews. Given my definition, you would conclude that being global then is a way of thinking. Travelling and experience may enhance global awareness, but the way of thinking takes precedence."

His advice to recent graduates stepping out into the world is, "The world is opening up. All the big corporations talk about fierce competition for talent in Africa and Asia. As a recent graduate I would see this as a good thing. Do well in your chosen field, but also take time to read broadly about the world."

People who are hiring want problem solvers, so critical thinking or problem solving skills are extremely important. If your study program does not provide ample opportunity for this, do team sports, join an organisation, or start a club with your friends. You will learn much from these experiences."

Palvi Shah

PALVI is from Kenya and is of Indian ethnicity. She has lived and worked in India (Bangalore), USA (New York) and UK (London). Palvi moved back to Nairobi after living in the UK for 14 years, to take on the Regional East Africa CFO role at Africa Internet Holding (AIH) - an e-commerce start up (Jumia and related websites) in Kenya. She says, "I always knew I would get involved with business; I guess it was because I grew up in a family where most of the extended family (my father and his siblings) were involved in running the family business. At school I was good at both arts and sciences, but decided not to pursue the sciences further."

Palvi went to the University of Warwick in the UK to study Law and Business Studies, and graduated in 2002 with a BA. Because she did a part law degree, she briefly considered pursuing law, but during her studies, she quickly realised that business interested her more, so she looked at careers in banking, consulting and assurance, and settled into pursuing a chartered accountancy qualification. Looking back, she says, "At the time, I felt that all of these would be good ways to get exposure to the business world. However, over time, I have also become more interested in development economics and private sector development projects. This has been partly responsible for my move back to Africa, and in time, I believe I will probably try to apply my skill set in this area."

Palvi decided to do the full time MBA programme at London Business School and she graduated in 2013. Having graduated from the MBA, she made the choice to move back to Africa, and looked for opportunities there. The AIH position was advertised on the London Business School career website and looked interesting to her, so she applied for it. She also considered other opportunities; speaking to a number of private equity firms for example. In the end she interviewed with AIH and they had the best offer to make, so she decided to take it on.

Most of her pre-MBA career was spent at BDO LLP in London, where she trained as a Chartered Accountant and remained until she was an Audit Manager and decided she wanted to expand her horizons. Palvi shares that a move into the finance industry is very typical for a lot of ACAs coming out of practice. She also essentially did just that, but took a detour to fit in the MBA along the way.

After leaving the audit lifestyle behind, Palvi had no

intention or inclination to go back into Finance. However, she thinks her current role will offer great exposure to the East African markets. She says, "Being in a start-up environment allows me to build systems and controls and finance teams almost from scratch, so I believe it will be interesting and challenging."

One critical thing from her past role that has prepared Palvi for her current one, is the fact that the technical nature of her previous job is directly relevant in her current job.

In addition to this, other most useful skill sets such as Project Management, people skills, leadership, teamwork and communication have come in handy. She says, "I started to develop all of these at BDO, and continued to do so during the MBA. In the job I do, these skills are almost more useful than the technical skills, as a big part of the job is all about leadership."

Commenting on her greatest career highlight and her future career path, Palvi says: "I had a very satisfactory career at BDO: my career to date has been very short in the grand scheme of things. I feel like most of it is still ahead of me. In the immediate future I want to stay on in Africa and see what I can do here. In the longer term, we'll see." We can only watch out for this smart and purposeful young woman.

For Palvi, there is no specific 'First global encounter.' She feels that her outlook has always been global. She rhetorically asks, "How can it not, when I am part of an Indian family that has lived in Kenya for 3+ generations?" Palvi also had the privilege to travel since she was very young, and Kenya has also always been a tourist destination. So, she encountered people from different parts of the world from an early age. In addition to these, all of her schooling was at a British school, where at the time, the majority of her teachers were expatriates.

Palvi's thinking in a global direction has been influenced first by her family, who have always been open-minded and encouraging. The extensive travelling she did with her family from her early years has encouraged her to continue travelling, exploring and meeting people from around the world. Later in life, she spent 8 months living and working in Bangalore as part of an AIESEC exchange. The people she met in Bangalore were from very diverse backgrounds and lived in different parts of the world. This experience made her realise that she loves meeting people from around the world. Some of those people are amongst her best friends now.

Having travelled extensively to a number of places across the Far East, Latin America, USA, Europe and Africa, the three most important things she has learnt on her travels are:

- A much better level of self-awareness, because in most of these situations you are in a strange place with strange people and you learn about how you cope and deal with these things.
- Related to the above, she observed you learn to trust that things will eventually work out.
- You learn to be open-minded to new ideas and people.

Palvi's global outlook is driven by the fact that her best friends are scattered around the world, and technology allows her to connect with them daily. She points out; "It is impossible to remain cocooned in a local mindset." Most of Palvi's global collaborations and experiences have been via AIESEC and interacting with the London Business School Network.

To succeed globally, Palvi agrees that one needs to be open-minded, self-aware, know what you want, and demonstrate boldness.

The skills and attitudes she has brought to the table, which has given her an edge over others, are: being open and honest about what she thinks, and trying to avoid the follow-the-crowd mentality, but rather telling herself that it is okay if she is different from everyone else around her. Also, without feeling obliged to tow someone else's line, she has been free to pursue her own path.

Dedication, perseverance, hard work and optimism are some of the attitudes Palvi displays regularly, and these have served her well on her journey. She however had to learn quickly how to work well with different people. She says, "I have a certain style of working and communicating. I learned very early on that this needs adapting depending, on who you work with." And moving forward, she wants to keep building her leadership skills.

As for the challenges of being in a global environment, Palvi points out, "It does not matter how many times you do it, it never gets easier to say goodbye to friends and family, and pick up and move somewhere else – even though you know there is a good reason you are doing it."

When it comes to who a global graduate is, and, what she would look for if she were hiring a recent graduate, Palvi says, "The main thing about someone global is someone with an open-minded outlook on everything." Her advice to recent graduates about to step out into the world is, "Work out what you want, and then work out how you can get there. Obstacles do exist, but there is almost always a way. And remember, people are always willing to help you: you can always ask. The worst someone can do is say no."

Will she do it all over again? Palvi says, "Maybe, but I don't think about it much. The path I have chosen has given me a lot of satisfaction, despite challenges. And I don't think the grass is greener on the other side."

Dr Tillmann Schneider

FROM being a paramedic for his Zivildienst (the former compulsory paid national service in Germany), to earning a PhD in Law, Tillmann hasn't always followed a straight set path to his current position. He has worked in Germany, Brazil, Italy, China, Ghana and Sierra Leone.

Tillmann is from Emlichheim, a place he describes as "something between a village and a small city in the middle of nowhere." He recalls it as a peaceful, but boring place when he was growing up. He always knew there was a big world waiting for him.

Without being really sure about what to study, he started to study law in the small German city of Osnabrück, but left two years later to continue in the capital Berlin.

As part of his course, he had to undertake an internship, so he travelled to Salvador in Brazil to do so. This was his first long distance travel, although he had spent some of his childhood holidaying in Italy and France.

Tillmann later sat for the state exam and came 5th out of 700 students, something he would like to be mute about, but I think it is pretty impressive. He first toyed with the idea of going to further his studies in the USA, but that required him getting a grant for that study period and it also meant waiting for another year and half before he could get on the grant programme like many other German lawyers.

Not sure whether he should start his pupillage in law, he moved to Rome instead. However, his stay in Rome didn't quite work out, so he returned to Germany and completed his pupillage in Hamburg. This involved going through different stages of state courts, administration and private law firms.

After finishing his legal education, he worked for a short time in a law firm in the area of energy law, but didn't feel happy. Therefore, he was happy to be accepted as part of a graduate research group to start working on a PhD thesis. Part of his PhD was to work in Ghana for six months, to access judgements. He says that he was keen to be at a destination longer than usual, and he got the chance to come to Ghana at a time when the country was doing relatively well and seen as the 'rising star'.

After working on his PhD for three years, he took time

out to work for GTZ, now GIZ, (Gesellschaft für Internationale Zusammenarbeit) or the German Agency for Development Cooperation in Sierra Leone, for two-and-a half years. Tillmann returned to Germany to finish his PhD, and is now working as a freelance consultant in the area of Law and Development, with emphasis on anti-corruption and human rights.

When I asked if it was competitive to access the jobs in West Africa, he said that the work on his PhD thesis gave him a competitive advantage. Tillmann thinks that getting the job in Sierra Leone was also a matter of the right timing, because GIZ needed somebody urgently. More importantly, not everyone was keen to go to work in Sierra Leone, a country that was recovering from war. Even worse, the person before him had left, six months into the job.

Tillmann's global collaborations are diverse: his former company GIZ is in itself a global company. He has also had global exchanges on academic conferences, and with colleagues from other international organisations. Some of these conferences have taken him to the UK, The Netherlands and Mozambique. Tillmann says, "A mix of curiosity and respect is crucial for any useful exchange to succeed, especially in a global context." He however notes that there is also space for disagreement, as differences in opinions are not always a bad thing.

When it comes to global experiences, Tillmann likes meeting different people and living in different cultural settings, because, "It changes and shakes your conviction of what is normal or not normal." One of Tillmann's most influential experiences was when he went to Rome. This was a turning point in his life, because things so far had always worked out, but in Rome they did not, mainly because he failed to prepare for opportunities beforehand. The lesson he learnt from this experience is, "To be prepared to manage failure and grow." Still, he doesn't think that planning has to be an absolute 100 percent, because preparation is a continuous process.

He describes his valuable skills as being a quick learner and a good listener, who is able to analyse and filter information. He is particularly good at analysing problems and situations. Tillmann is also good at negotiating, and is able to organise prior research before the start of a project. These are all useful skills to survive everywhere. Tillmann adds that, having the confidence to provide advice to national high-level partners and, having good managerial skills are additional skills he has brought to the table to get ahead.

Moving forward, he wants to improve on his strategic networking skills and diplomatic communication, as he often says things as they are, sometimes a little too bluntly. Tillmann advises others not to underestimate the power of language, because knowing different languages is an essential skill for a global graduate. He sees successful people as those who are able to anticipate change, and he further advises that one should always analyse market logic and foresee opportunities.

One of the challenges Tillmann found working in some global environments, for instance in a foreign country like Sierra Leone was the challenge of being accepted as a younger boss. He observed that although hierarchy is sometimes necessary, working with it could be a major challenge.

Tillmann strongly believes that to be a global graduate, one must keep in mind that "Graduation is certainly not the end of school, because it is a continuous process of interacting with people." His simple, but loaded advice to every graduate is, "Dare!"

Catalina Geib

CATALINA is half Peruvian and half German, and grew up in Luxembourg. With a background as hers, it will have been easy to guess that Catalina might have started her global journey early. But it was actually the time she spent in London that she recalls to be her first global encounter. She says, "When I went to London and broke out of the bubble that was Luxembourg, I really believed that I was on top of the world going to university at the heart of London, crossing the Waterloo Bridge and seeing its iconic monuments. The fast pace and the cosmopolitan feel to the city really made me believe that I have stepped further into a global outlook in my career."

Catalina did not have to look very far to set her eyes on a global career path, as most of her friends and family, who had embarked on international careers, inspired her to take on the same path. Many of her family members in Peru left the country to study and work in the United States and seek better opportunities there.

Catalina's undergraduate degree at King's College London was in European Studies, with a focus on political economy. After she graduated, she immediately started an MSc in Political Economy of Late Development at the London School of Economics. This postgraduate degree consisted of an interdisciplinary approach between economic history and development studies.

Catalina has worked in Luxembourg, Germany, Brussels, the United Kingdom and Peru, and now works in the United States. She currently works in the External Relations Department at the Inter-American Development Bank. She is assigned to the solidarity unit, which deals with the relations with community based organisations that support underserved Latino communities in the Washington DC area. Her job is to coordinate and organize fundraising campaigns that are held internally at the bank.

Getting to her current role, Catalina points out, was reasonably competitive. Since a German foundation, together with the German government fund the placement, only few people are able to receive this fellowship. It is relatively less competitive than applications for the private sector or directly applying at the international institution.

Long before heading to United States, she worked for an NGO in Lima, Peru, conducting and writing a business plan for them. Even before that, Catalina worked at the European Research Council Executive Agency in Brussels. At Brussels, she worked in the Director's Office and worked closely with the Secretary General of the European Research Council, in order to analyse and support their internationalisation strategy.

Catalina has definitely learnt a lot along the way, to be in her current position. She shares, "During my role at the European Research Council Executive Agency, I learnt how to be more careful and definitely more precise in my communication to colleagues and people outside the bank. It is very important to be clear in everything you communicate and do, in order to avoid unnecessary misunderstandings and problems. Moreover, my previous roles showed me how to use Excel more effectively, and how best to prioritize tasks in order to become more efficient. Motivating myself and persevering is what I learnt during my role as a campaigner in Germany in 2009."

Although studying in London was Catalina's "real" global encounter, thinking global is a given. Catalina says, "A global mindset is innate in me." Because of growing up in a multicultural environment and travelling since she was little, she thought globally from the start. And through her education she has learnt how to break through boundaries and be constantly curious.

Catalina's travels have been widely across Europe, the US and Peru. She has learnt how to be open and curious about new cultures and customs, while tolerating different perceptions and focusing on the positive things and the advantages of each place.

Her global collaborations are equally diverse. She has been on scientific council meetings with attendees from across Europe, to even more serious projects such as working at the European Commission in Brussels (the European Research Council Executive Agency), where she was also involved in fundraising for a project, in a collaborative effort between three other coordinators who were also doing their traineeship at the European commission. Catalina has also worked hard in a fun environment with co-workers and supervisors from many different countries, helping on the merchandise stand on a Robbie Williams European tour, in order to earn extra money.

Catalina didn't just earn money from these collaborations: she learnt that "Different nationalities have different ideas about teamwork and work in general. It is hard to overcome the differences in mindsets at first, but the willingness to understand and openness helps."

Catalina's global outlook is driven by this belief, "It is not enough to live and work in a bubble or in a comfort zone. Although I haven't been in an environment that is in complete opposition to my own, this is what I am still striving to achieve: always breaking the bubble, looking for new opportunities and seizing them; constantly growing, to understand what I am good at and what I really want in life. My supportive family and friends, as well as the new people that I meet, are always inspirational and a great support network."

I cannot imagine Catalina missing out on any past or present opportunities as a result of not being strategically global in her outlook. But Catalina insightfully suggests that she thinks she missed the opportunity to receive a different kind of education. This is because, if she had mastered the courage to leave the comfort zone that was London, by applying to places in graduate school in the United States, then she missed her chance to receive a different kind of education that might have been more thorough and different from her own, as well as the best education in the world.

Nevertheless, she says, "I still believe that I have taken full advantage of all opportunities that were laid before me." To compete and succeed globally, Catalina thinks, "One has to know more than two languages. Chances are, you need them for international employers, and it shows that you are open to new cultures and can adapt easily in certain circumstances." Catalina's global edge, amongst other things comes from being friendly, learning the customs and mentality of different cultures in order to avoid misunderstandings, and more importantly, trying to understand how business is done by knowing what norms are utilised for different situations.

Catalina had to learn to be patient in certain situations. She explains, "Sometimes, especially in big institutions that are very political, it is important to understand that things move and function a certain way which cannot be changed from one day to the next. I also had to learn how to be very focused and concentrate on every single step I take. Lastly, they say that the devil is in the detail – that is very true, so I had to learn how to pay extreme attention to detail (these are things you don't necessarily learn at university)."

The skills that Catalina would like to learn to demonstrate more of are: first, she would definitely like to acquire more technical skills. Next would be to show more of her presentation skills and perfect her writing skills too. Catalina says she is very aware of the fact that she needs to improve her numerical skills. I know with her positive and proactive attitude, she is well on track.

"Being open, friendly, helpful and proactive" are the key attributes that have seen Catalina through. Catalina mentions that it is important to be a giver rather than a taker. She says, "Helping others, and giving advice to others along the way, will help build a good network of people which is much more rewarding and fulfilling than just taking all the time."

Catalina would want to stay in her current department of External Relations, but she would like to switch teams where she could learn and write more, as well as understand the projects of the bank in more detail, and in the process, continue to understand where her real strengths are.

Catalina's greatest career highlight is more in the present. She lives in such a global city, Washington D.C., and she works for an institution that has many opportunities and where interesting people work. She says of her role, "I feel very privileged, and I am certain that with hard work, this experience can take me somewhere even more exciting." And I could not agree more.

One of Catalina's challenges, as a result of being global, is that people and friends leave to take on different jobs in cities across the globe. It is a fast paced environment and people rarely stay in one place for a long period of time. She would like to have all these friends in one place, but that not being possible, she needs to learn how to keep in touch with them even if they are far away.

Being a big learner, what would Catalina look for when she is hiring a global graduate? She states, "There is a saying that I like: "Think globally, act locally". More than having a global mindset I would also be interested whether that person has supported his or her own community through volunteering and doing community work."

Her advice to graduates is, "Don't be afraid to fail. Follow your passions. Step outside of your comfort zone and don't forget to keep in touch with your friends: they are a great support network when things get more difficult."

This advice comes from a very personal place, because Catalina had to get rid of her own fears and trust herself more. She says, "Had I believed in myself more, I would have chosen an economics class from the first year onwards, in order to learn economic policy afterwards." Regardless of past fears and choices, Catalina is well on track to go places and make an impact.

Selase Kanda

RIGHT after his high school education, Selase took a job as a Stock Controller and Office Assistant at a private clinic where his father worked. These roles were perfect training grounds and a way to acquire transferable skills. At the clinic, he learnt how to make use of Excel sheets to capture data into a database, something he continues to find useful in the workplace.

With a Bachelors in Administration (Accounting option) at the University of Ghana, followed by a Master's in Financial Economics at the University of Manchester

- which he recently completed, Selase says he did not always know what he wanted to do, but his career pursuits shifted as he went along in education and work.

Very early in his undergraduate studies, he considered pursuing an accounting career. He then shifted to Finance later during his undergraduate studies: although he still majored in Accounting, with a first class degree, he decided to pursue a professional investment course called the Chartered Financial Analyst programme. After undergraduate studies, he additionally decided to pursue a Master's with a mix of Finance and Economics as a means to acquire some quantitative skills for technical finance roles.

Luckily, Selase doesn't recount making any career choices he would consider bad. He thinks his career choice is a good one, as he got exposed early to working in the investment division of a bank, specifically in asset management. This experience gave him a clearer perspective on specific areas in Finance he would want to work in. He also had to take on two roles at the same time early in his work at the bank, which polished his multitasking skills.

Although Selase is just starting out his global career, he says if he had to do it all over again and differently, he would use time more wisely and effectively in building himself and his attitude.

He started off as a National Service personnel at a bank, and he was retained after the national service period. According to him, "I wouldn't consider it competitive, because I was recommended by a former school mate for the job." Selase must have done something right, because not every national service person was retained.

Even though Selase mentioned he did not always have a global mindset, I wanted to know if there was any one person, thing or situation that has influenced his thinking in a global direction. To this, Selase says, "One of my main influences to think in a global direction was the exposure I received at SPEC Consult Limited, which broadened my horizon from thinking narrowly, and made me try to meet a global standard." SPEC Consult Limited is a company whose founder is the author of this book.

His first 'real' global encounter was during his pursuit of postgraduate studies, where he interacted with people from all over the world on his programme of study. Prior to that, he was offered a place at the International Students' hostel on campus in the final year of his undergraduate study. He learnt a lot from his Japanese room-mate and had the opportunity to interact closely with other international students.

Of his experience while studying in the UK, he says he learnt so much in a year. His two main learning experiences are:

1. That hard work and ethical behaviour are necessary for a healthy and thriving business environment.
2. Building on knowledge is key, and in that respect, developed countries take education and research extremely seriously.

The main challenge Selase faced in a global environment was adapting from simply listening at lectures to asking questions in order to seek a deeper understanding, and challenge the status quo. His new drive for a global outlook, is driven by the desire to be competitive everywhere. Selase says in order for one to succeed everywhere, "I believe it takes being knowledge-hungry, having the right attitude, as well as hard work, to succeed globally. During my Master's, I realized that hard work was key, as there was no room for slack." He also does not give up easily when he sets his mind to do something. This is a very healthy attitude he has adopted, that has given him an edge over others.

A sense of curiosity, motivation and the desire to excel tend to be Selase's constant state of mind, and these have helped him on his journey. The skill he had to learn quickly was to be a problem solver, no matter the constraints on his job as an Investment Officer. Moving forward, he would like to be more resilient and take more initiative.

According to Selase, a global graduate is a person who is well prepared to work and excel in any global environment, or to adapt suitably to deliver in such an environment. If he was recruiting one, he would look out for traits of uncompromising industriousness, good communication and interpersonal skills, ethics and professionalism, as well as a willingness to learn and be teachable.

Selase intends to advance himself further through strategic knowledge acquisition and positioning and his advice to graduates the world over is, "To thrive for excellence; build on knowledge; be the best you can in any given situation; never disappoint; and always leave a solid impression."

Lindsay Bayham

With Lindsay in Accra

SOME people spend hours on the social media site Facebook, commenting on status updates, tagging and liking pictures of people they know or do not know, but Lindsay did spend some of her time using her global expertise to work with Facebook's research team.

Lindsay recalls being eager to travel on her own after hearing stories about her dad's international experiences. Her first experience abroad came when, as a high school student, her choir took a tour to Vienna, Austria and Prague (in the Czech Republic). Lindsay thinks the experience was a sheltered one, because she was part of a tour group. However, her first 'real' experience on her own was as an exchange student in Germany, the summer after she graduated from high school.

She lived with a family in a small town in Eastern Germany and spoke only German for nearly a month. She remembers feeling very excited to connect so well with her host family, particularly her host sister, while speaking another language.

Lindsay studied Public Policy for her undergraduate degree (BA), at Duke University in North Carolina. Her graduate studies were in Sociology, at the University of California-Berkeley. She is currently working on her PhD at the same world-class university. She says her greatest career highlight is, "Starting graduate school and receiving my MA. Although that's an educational highlight, it's part of my academic career track."

Lindsay does a combination of things: takes classes; does a lot of reading and writing; designs research projects; and mentors undergraduate students. In addition to all of these, she also tries to stay involved in different forms of activism or consulting on the side. In the future, she will also teach.

Being prudent, Lindsay applied for a position in different graduate departments, and she chose Berkeley because she was interested in working with a few specific professors there. Lindsay is quick to point out how extremely competitive it was getting into Berkley, because, like most top graduate programs — out of 400 students who applied to Berkeley, only about 30 were admitted. She was only accepted at 2 out of the 6 schools she applied to. Lindsay thinks the reason in part might be because, "I did not have much prior experience in sociology."

Lindsay says, "I always knew that I was interested in research, but I didn't really consider academia as a career path until after I had graduated from college. During college, I thought about becoming a human rights lawyer, especially after I worked for a human rights lawyer. I also wanted to do research for a large non-profit or NGO such as the Brookings Institution. I realized, however, that most of the people doing research work, had gone to graduate school first."

When I asked Lindsay whether she always knew what she wanted to do, just like most people, she replied, "I did not always want to be an academic (professor). In fact, it was only after I graduated from college that I realized that I wanted to devote my career to teaching and research. After my senior year of college, I spent a year in Ghana doing research on a Fulbright Fellowship. That experience inspired me to work on anti-corruption issues, so I spent the following year working at an NGO focused on international policy. While I was at the NGO, I realized that I missed the hands-on process of original research, where I got to talk to people and connect their responses to broader social patterns. I also realized that much of the research that the NGO I worked for needed was actually contracted out to professors and graduate students outside of the NGO. I therefore decided that I should go to graduate school if I wanted to do more original research."

Lindsay mapped out her career path and worked as a research assistant for two professors at Duke University—one a historian, the other a human rights lawyer. Lindsay also worked as a research intern for former President Jimmy Carter's foundation; The Carter Center's Access to Information Program in Atlanta.

Commenting on what she learnt from her past roles, she says "It exposed my interest in doing research and made me realize that I would never be happy working a "desk job" where I didn't get to ask questions, talk to people, and analyze broader social patterns. In that sense, my prior roles channelled my longstanding interest in social justice into a very clear career pathway."

Lindsay also mentions that other past roles showed her, "How to work with different types of people, particularly those who might be a bit more demanding or brusque in their personal interactions. I've learned not to take criticism too personally, otherwise it can diminish your motivation and willingness to keep working towards your goals." Lindsay adds that, she is still working on this and knows it is a never-ending learning curve.

Lindsay's dad played a big part in orienting her towards global events. He was a Business Coordinator for a large medical products company and took many international business trips. Lindsay's dad had also taken a year-long trip around the world when he was in his early 20's. He shared many stories with her and her younger sister about how the rest of the world was different from the United States.

As a high school student, Lindsay was interested in learning more about other cultures and countries, so she started volunteering at the International Institute of St. Louis, a refugee resettlement organisation in her hometown that sponsored many international awareness events. Through volunteering, she not only learned a little bit more about what was going on in the rest of the world, but she also got to actually interact with people from the different countries, something she otherwise would not have had the chance to do in most of her daily life as a student.

However, once Lindsay reached college, her mentor, a professor and human rights lawyer, further influenced her. She was originally South African who had been an anti-Apartheid activist in her youth. She says of her mentor, "She nurtured my conviction that people everywhere deserve a basic level of dignity, and she showed me how I might channel that conviction into meaningful work with people from other countries and cultures."

Lindsay has worked long-term in Ghana and the US, and has been involved in in-depth collaborations in both Ghana and South Africa, mostly for research and conferences. In Ghana, she worked with researchers and NGOs to understand why people choose to emigrate from the country, what the consequences are for Ghana, and how particular social policies and media campaigns might affect people's migration decisions. Lindsay also collaborated with an NGO to promote youth civic engagement and volunteerism in Kumasi, in the Ashanti Region of Ghana.

She also worked with a professor and the South African Constitutional Court to understand how ordinary South Africans related to the South African Constitution and the Constitutional Court building.

Commenting on some of the key learning points from these collaborations, Lindsay says, "Collaborations are hard!

The various experiences I've had working with other people have taught me just how difficult it is to compromise. It's easy to talk about respecting other viewpoints and taking other perspectives into consideration, but when you're working on a project that you really care about, it's hard to give up your ideas if you really think that they will give you the best chance for success. I've had to learn how to prioritize my ideas and fight for only those that I think are most important. But I've also had to learn how to get out of my head enough to understand why other people might think differently. It can be hard to do this if you and your collaborators disagree on fundamental things like personal values and goals for the project; it's a bit easier if you agree on goals, but diverge on how best to get there. But even when you and your collaborators have different values, it's important to find some similarities from which you can build a successful partnership."

Knowing Lindsay, her global collaborations list will grow taller. So far Lindsay has lived in, studied in, or travelled to Austria, the Czech Republic, Germany, The Netherlands, Belgium, Turkey, Brazil, Kenya, Togo, South Africa, Morocco and Ghana. She always learns something from every travel experience, even if it is something about herself. With each trip, she says, "I gain experience dealing with unfamiliar situations — how to problem-solve in crises, for example, and how to relate to people without knowing very much about them."

Some of the challenges of being in a global environment are the fact that things are changing very rapidly in many ways. Not only are country-level policies changing (e.g. trade and tax policies), but the social infrastructure of many countries is rapidly shifting as well. In Ghana, for example, an increasing number of her friends and contacts have migrated abroad to take advantage of opportunities for work or education. On a personal level, this means she has to constantly develop new relationships, because the social landscape looks a little different every time she returns to Ghana.

Lindsay mentions she always had a somewhat global orientation thanks to her dad's experiences, which developed her global 'mindset'. She says when she started travelling on her own, however, "I felt like I have learned how to listen and relate to people from almost any cultural or religious background, and how to problem-solve on the fly when I need to. I also feel like I'm more aware of how differences can be resources in cooperating and solving a problem."

Lindsay's global outlook is also driven by the strong belief that the world is always changing, and is becoming - in some ways - more integrated. She thinks "it will be ever more necessary to be aware of alternative perspectives and ways of organizing markets and societies in the future." As an American, Lindsay thinks "Americans can be quite insular and self-focused, and travelling abroad has shown me how much more aware of global trends and politics, people from other countries are."

Commenting on what it takes to succeed globally, and how she has done it, Lindsay says, "I think you have to be open, curious, and flexible, so that you don't miss an opportunity to learn from someone or some situation. It also helps if you actively seek ways to challenge yourself and push yourself out of your comfort zone in terms of projects, skills, and habits. You also can't take yourself too seriously, which means being able to accept criticism constructively, and being able to escape your own point of view and believe that someone else's perspective might be equally valid."

One of Lindsay's prized skills is being willing to listen, which other people appreciate. Listening to others not only tunes Lindsay in to their expectations, but it also helps build personal rapport. Lindsay says "she tries not to make people feel like their perspectives are strange or 'weird' in any way, which puts people at ease and makes them more comfortable with contributing."

In spite of the above skill, Lindsay had to 'learn how to learn quickly.' As an academic, she says, "I am often asked to comment on topics which I know little about, and sometimes I am asked to problem-solve in situations where I have very little experience. I have to be able to find information (whether through other people or more formal sources), synthesize it quickly into an actionable plan, and convince others that my plan is a good one. I've also had to learn (the hard way!) to accept criticism while not taking it too seriously - that is, being reflective enough to acknowledge that I can do things better, while still maintaining a level of self-esteem and confidence that keeps me motivated to move forward on my goals."

In the future, Lindsay would like to learn more tech skills, such as how to design a website or query a database to analyse data. Although she does not think that tech knowledge can ever replace good ideas and basic critical thinking skills, it is becoming more and more useful to know how to work with computer systems and big data, particularly in analytical or research-based fields (whether in academia or the business world).

Lindsay's advice to graduates is, "People in business respond to others with whom they're comfortable, and that often comes down to very specific forms of self-presentation and carriage. For people from all continents and backgrounds, I think it's important to understand who you'll be working with and where they're coming from, and taking the time to understand how your forms of personal presentation (ways of dressing, speaking, and behaving) might be interpreted. That's not to say that you need to change your behavior entirely to suit others, but at least be aware that other people might not understand exactly what you're trying to communicate, especially when you're communicating in subtle ways (e.g. with a certain type of clothing)."

According to Lindsay, "a global graduate is someone who has taken initiative to learn more about other parts of the world, and who makes an active effort to stay on top of major economic, political, and social developments worldwide. He or she is curious and flexible, takes initiative to develop and follow up on his or her ideas, and can think quickly on his or her feet." These and more are qualities Lindsay would look for, if she were hiring a recent graduate.

Dalia Mankauskas

"I always knew what I wanted to do, but I've changed my mind about that a few times." Most of us can identify with that profound statement. Dalia has a BA in Economics and a Master's in Banking from the University of Vilnius, Lithuania.

Dalia first thought she wanted to work in Human Resources, but she moved into the Banking sector and finally ended up as an interpreter, a career she absolutely loves.

When Dalia finally decided that working in a bank was actually not for her, she started exploring other possibilities.

Someone suggested interpreting. Dalia says interpreting is a very competitive career path, as the need for interpreters is not that great in her native Lithuania. However, Dalia knew that if you undertake and finish proper studies as she has done (Dalia also has a special certificate for Interpreting) and you are patient enough – it all works out.

Before becoming a freelance interpreter and an interpreting trainer at a University, Dalia's journey was shaped by AIESEC, where she held a number of positions in this student-run organisation. She confirms it was the best training ground for "the real world." Dalia also had other major roles in a human resources company working on various HR projects, in a major global bank, as Portfolio Credit Risk Analyst.

Dalia says there have been some useful lessons along the way, which have prepared her for her current role as an interpreter. She recounts, "The interesting thing about interpreting is that everything you have ever learned will become handy one day. Interpreters need to have a very broad general knowledge, so everything you've done before interpreting counts. For example, for the most part I really didn't enjoy my time at the bank, but now I feel much more comfortable interpreting all sorts of presentations on banking, on economy or on the Euro (a very popular subject these days)."

Dalia credits her parents for getting her to think in a global direction. Although, her parents grew up in the Soviet Union (for the first eight years of her life she did too), they travelled quite a lot and were constantly telling stories of these places far away. Her parents would always encourage her sister and her to go to other countries if they had the chance. She says of her parents, "It all seemed natural at a time, but now that I think of it, my parents were quite extraordinary in that sense."

Her first clear memory of travelling is going to Germany with her family. "I must have been 11 or 12 years old, and Germany seemed quite magical to me and yet not too different from home. That's something I keep remembering while abroad, that there are people living in all these places and they are just the same as I am. It's just that their life is a little bit different in some ways, though for the most part it's exactly the same."

Apart from Lithuania, Dalia has lived and worked in Ghana for a year, and in two other countries: the USA for one year, and Turkey for two months.

Her travels cover a big part of Europe, the USA, and a few countries in Africa, Hong Kong and China.

All these places had a great influence on Dalia's personality. It taught her tolerance, patience and appreciation for her life, just to name a few. The global collaborations she has been involved in are varied and ongoing. In her current job, collaborating with people from abroad is a given. As an interpreter, it is her job to ensure smooth communication between languages and cultures. Each assignment, to her, is a form of a global collaboration.

Her past role with AIESEC, which is a global student organisation present in more than 100 countries, meant everything the organisation did had a global component. At AIESEC, they were organising internships abroad, had international members in their national teams, organising and participating in a number of conferences every year.

Some of these conferences made huge impressions on her. Particularly, the meetings of all AIESEC national boards: one in India where she was representing Lithuania, and the other in Poland, where she was representing Ghana. She recalls the amazing experience of a gathering of more than 500 people from all over the world in one place.

After AIESEC, Dalia also organised a conference for a local NGO, which invited people from all around the world. Her responsibility was to take care of 20 Roma people from Hungary. It is an experience she learnt a lot from.

She recounts, "The thing that keeps striking me again and again is the fact that people in general are the same wherever you go. They may have some cultural background that is different from me, but in many ways they are quite the same. Therefore I can't understand how someone can be intolerant of other nationalities, races, ethnicity etc."

Even with all these impactful global collaborations, Dalia modestly says,

"I am not sure I can claim that I have succeeded globally, but I would say that what you need is determination, patience, tolerance and communication. If you want to achieve something more in your life than just working in the same place for 40 years, earning the same salary and being 'secure', then you'll have to put in a lot of hard work and the four qualities I've listed are a must."

On what Dalia has brought to the table, and the edge she has over others, she says,

"I think my 'edge' over others is that I do everything to the best of my abilities. And that is very important, because there are so many people in the world who just want to do what they like doing, what they enjoy doing, and they claim, "I can do those things well, but I don't like doing other things, so I won't." That's just wrong. You have to learn to enjoy what you do, as well as manage to do the work you don't enjoy."

Tolerance is the skill and attitude she had to learn quickly. Dalia recalls when she went to the USA as an exchange student at age 15, and found that the life there was quite different from the one she had known. It was there that she met African-Americans and openly gay people for the first time, which at the time was quite unheard of in Lithuania or perhaps in her surroundings.

Even though Dalia's work is all about communication, making sure that communication runs smoothly is not always very easy. For instance, "One thing in one language and or culture may mean a totally different thing in another." This is a challenge Dalia faces, working in her kind of global environment.

According to Dalia, a global graduate should have a broad understanding on what is happening in the world and how everything is connected. He or she should be a person ready to think and act outside the box. If she is hiring one, she would be looking for someone with creativity, and a willingness to learn: someone who simply has a broader outlook of the world.

Dalia's advice is to African graduates, because from her time in Ghana, she says, "I noticed something that some Ghanaian graduates were lacking. They were unable to show their personality. Somehow, students want to be like everybody else, to do what everybody else does, afraid to be different in any way. Don't be afraid to be yourself, to be different, to live the life you want to live, not the one somebody told you to have." I couldn't agree more with Dalia, as I have lost count of the number of times I have had to tell graduates at some of my training sessions to learn to be their own person and step away from the mob mentality.

Dalia makes it clear she won't change anything on her journey, if she had to do it all over again, because, "Without one step, another step could not have been taken."

Dr Elvis Adjei

ELVIS is Ghanaian, but he resides in the United Kingdom. He always had a dream of being an international player, but he was not quite sure where exactly the opportunity was to come from. He carefully chose his postgraduate degree programmes to reflect what he wanted to do.

Elvis had only two career paths in mind: either to work with an international bank, or to be a Research Economist with an international financial or development institution such as the IMF, World Bank or African Development Bank. Being in academia was the least on his list of preferences, in spite of the research element embedded in an academic career.

Interestingly, Elvis was a full time Postdoctoral Lecturer at the Bangor University of Wales, UK, where his primary tasks in this role were in the areas of teaching and research. He specialised in Economics, Banking and Finance, with a large amount of teaching focus in Quantitative and Statistical Methods.

Elvis is also a regular Visiting Lecturer on the modular programme of the Graduate Institute of Management and Public Administration (GIMPA), Ghana, where he teaches Managerial Finance and Business Economics on these programmes.

Getting into the role at Bangor was very competitive. He shares, "I applied for the role when I was then an International Consultant for the African Development Bank in Tunisia. I was short-listed and invited for an interview a month after the application deadline, so I needed to be in the United Kingdom at my own cost for the interview. I returned to Tunisia a day after the interview to continue with my consultancy work while hoping that I would be successful in the interview I had just attended.

Knowing the large number of students who had just completed their PhD programmes in the United Kingdom at the peak of the financial recession, I had to count myself blessed to have been invited for an interview. The University needed only one person to occupy the position and I was the one offered the job two weeks after returning to Tunisia."

Elvis studied Tourism at The University of Cape Coast (Ghana) for his undergraduate degree; International Banking & Development Finance for his Master's; Economics for his PhD; and Teaching & Supporting Learning in Higher

Education for his PGCertHE, all from Bangor University of Wales. Elvis says, "The greatest highlight of my career is finding myself teaching and tutoring international and local students from all walks of life (Europeans, Americans, Asians, Africans…). It is a good feeling to know that I am impacting knowledge on my generation across the globe."

Elvis's past roles are:

- Project Officer - UT Financial Services Ltd. (now UT Bank), Ghana
- Credit Manager - UT Financial Services Ltd. (now UT Bank), Ghana
- Student Warden - Bangor University (UK)
- Administrative Support Assistant - Bangor University (UK)
- International Student Ambassador - Bangor University (UK)
- International Senior Warden - Bangor University (UK)
- Teaching Associate - Bangor University (UK)
- Tutor - Bangor University (UK)
- Visiting Lecturer - GIMPA (Ghana)
- International Consultant - African Development Bank (Tunisia).

Discipline, respect and commitment have been the three most important ingredients from Elvis's past roles, that have prepared him for his future roles. Having worked in a multicultural environment over the past few years, Elvis has come to appreciate the need to respect people and the way they respond to issues, from a global context. This is because he thinks this is the only way to work harmoniously with colleagues. Without this important ingredient, "Discipline and commitment alone cannot realise an organisation's objectives."

Elvis's first global encounter was when he left Ghana to pursue his Master's degree in the United Kingdom. He saw it as the best opportunity to meet other students from various parts of the globe, with unique experiences. This was how Elvis's global network started.

Elvis insightfully points out, "It is often said that we all live in a global village, and what affects a business environment in Asia has the tendency of affecting other businesses in Africa and elsewhere." In this light, it is no more appropriate to think in a 'black box'. Hence, the spillover effect, he says, has been the major driver that has influenced him to think from a global perspective.

Apart from living in Ghana, Tunisia and the United Kingdom, Elvis has also travelled to Cote d'Ivoire, Nigeria, Cameroon, Egypt, Turkey, Belgium, The Netherlands and Germany.

One thing he has learnt from these places is, "Always respect and accommodate other people's culture when in their environment." Elvis reckons this is the only way to foster good understanding.

Elvis says he always had a global mindset right from his university days at Cape Coast. He knew he would not only be operating within the confines of the Ghanaian environment, but would be actively involved with organisations that would expose him to the international stage. No wonder he took the initiative to apply for a position at the African Development Bank, whilst still an undergraduate.

Elvis knew that the African Development Bank, at the time, hired candidates only with a Master's degree and relevant experience, but he persevered. He got the opportunity to work with the Bank over a decade later. Elvis has been involved in various academic conferences and student recruitment programmes both in the United Kingdom and abroad. While he was doing his postgraduate course, Elvis used to be the International Student Ambassador on behalf of Bangor University, for Africa. He attended British Council recruitment fairs on behalf of Bangor University in Africa. He also attended and presented academic papers on very important conferences in Ghana, Tunisia and the United Kingdom.

Knowledge sharing and networking were the key learning points Elvis took from these global collaborations. Elvis is still in contact with some of the key persons he met on these meetings, which has eventually led to further academic collaborations.

A major driver that has influenced Elvis's global outlook is the fact that there is so much one can offer beyond his or her immediate environment. He says: "When I look at the human investment made on my own life, I would be denying my generation a great service if I were to think in a *black box*."

Elvis recognises that it takes a lot of hard work, commitment and focus to really be on top of one's game. He has always found a way to go the extra mile beyond what is expected of him. Elvis has the necessary skill-mix like multi-tasking, time management and using the appropriate econometric software packages. These same skills, he says, have been very relevant for consultancy assignments: they always give him the edge over others. He says, "These skills "have ultimately helped me to succeed globally."

With respect to what he has brought to the table, Elvis says he has a lot to share, but will rather focus on the feedback he gets from a large number of his students both in the UK and abroad, who enjoy his lectures due to his style of delivery and the patience he exhibits in his role. This has always translated into student satisfaction and impressive performance on the part of his students.

Elvis will want to demonstrate more of his leadership qualities due to the next phase of his career: He has taken on a new leadership role as a Principal of a College and it is very appropriate that he exhibits more of his leadership skills to inspire his team.

Despite the many challenges one can face in a global environment, Elvis's focus is on language barriers. This is because depending on where one finds him or herself, this can be a challenge. This has made him appreciate the need to be either bi- or multi-lingual. He says: "It can be so frustrating for a person to have an idea, yet cannot express him or herself, let alone convey the message. The opposite is also true when your recipients cannot understand you properly. Even if they do, sometimes the true meaning of the message is diluted due to the speaker's accent. To say that language barrier is the biggest challenge of being in a global environment is an understatement."

For Elvis, a global graduate is a graduate "Who thinks

outside the box, understands what goes on around the world and its recent events, beyond what he or she has been taught in the classroom or read in academic books." When it comes to hiring graduates, Elvis would most likely look for graduates who are able to apply academic concepts to real world scenarios and situations. This is the more reason why he favours scenario-based interviews, due to their ability of sifting out ordinary graduates from the best. Elvis points how, a graduate with a low grade, for instance, could give a better interview than a first class graduate due to their con-nection with the real world. In this case, a first class graduate could just be an ordinary graduate without any real world connection."

His advice goes to the Africans who have recently grad-uated or are about to step out into the world. "They should try to look out for volunteer jobs if they are unable to secure a paid job immediately after graduation. Quite a number of these graduates, sit at home doing nothing, only wonder-ing when they will get a well-paid job. At this point in their careers, they should focus more on enhancing their CVs, which could easily translate into more secured and well paid jobs in the future. A number of organisations, includ-ing the United Nations, are looking for volunteer workers. These cohorts of graduates or students should take advan-tage of these opportunities, as some could lead to permanent employment."

Looking back, he would not do anything differently, but instead, he would add more value to himself, if he were to do it all over again. Elvis wished he had done more volunteer jobs when he was a student, because these volunteer jobs come along with skills that one could never have learnt in the classroom. Additional language skills would be more appropriate if, he had to do it all over again.

Next for Elvis, is excelling in his new role as a Principal of a College that has opened in the United Kingdom. He is already excited for this new opportunity, because it will give him the chance to demonstrate his leadership skills as he envisages new challenges ahead.

Karen Tang

KAREN was born and raised in Taiwan. To date, she has lived on three different continents, worked in Europe (Paris and Hamburg) for a short period, and then in China for 5 years. She now lives and works in Canada for her current company's US office.

Karen has travelled to more than 20 countries: backpacked from Switzerland to Prague, taken a road trip with her mother to the north of Italy, and ridden a horse in Inner Mongolia. Karen says travel has been a valuable teacher - way more valuable than sitting in a classroom and learning about the world through someone else's eyes. She has learnt so much about the world and herself, through adventures, tears and laughter. But the most important lesson is that, "There's something about going far away from home that makes you really appreciate the place you live, and makes you want to explore your surroundings even more."

Although Karen did not always know what she wanted to do career-wise, some of the possible career paths she considered and also worked for, were International Hotel Chains, Travel Organizations, an Online Marketing Agency, and Internet companies in general.

With an MSc in eTourism from the University of Surrey in the UK, Karen is a Website Content Director for the leading Chinese Travel Website Qunar.com (NAS-DAQ:QUNR). Karen says that getting into her current role was not as competitive as it is for many others today. Karen took a calculated risk and decided to move to a new country, and looking back, she says, "I truly believe I made the correct decision at that time. I am lucky that I entered the market at a very early stage." She realised China would become an even more popular travel destination because of the upcoming Olympics at the time. She moved to Beijing in 2008 to join a start-up company (which is also her current company).

She was the first to join in 2008 in a junior marketing and public relations role. Her first promotion came after a year. Karen then became the Senior Marketing Manager for the company. She worked for the same company for almost 5 years (from 2008-2012), but she left the company at the end of 2012 because of some personal reasons. Karen rejoined the company in September 2013.

Her past experience in Marketing and Public Relations, as well as being part of the product marketing team, gave her a solid knowledge and understanding of user behaviour in the digital age; audience engagement, and building a fun and spirited team. All these have equally helped her in her current role as a Content and Marketing Director, as she needs to promote the company's brand via good quality editorial content, as well as improve user experience, and ultimately grow traffic.

Karen thinks that one of the main challenges of being in a global environment, is the rate of information explosion, which she sees as both complex and dynamic.

Her first real global encounter came in 2003 when she participated in an eTourism event in Helsinki, Finland, dubbed ENTER 2003, whilst on the Master's course at Surrey. She recalls, "It was an eye-opening experience."

Karen's global mindset was always being shaped by wanting to explore the world from every aspect, "From films, books, photography, the Internet and the most important-from having conversations with locals."

She mentions former CEO Fritz Demopoulos, as someone who had the most influence on her career and her general thinking in a global direction. Her current CEO C.C. Zhuang is also another influence. Karen says both men are great visionary entrepreneurs and great leaders she constantly learns from.

Karen's global outlook is driven by her need to create and influence the online travel space, because she believes innovation can change the way we travel, and the way we see the world.

Her global collaborations have involved different projects, from product development for the Four Seasons Hotel Chains, marketing promotions with Lonely Planet as well as collaborating with worldwide travel bloggers to create the best travel content.

Some of Karen's learning points from these collaborations are: "Prioritisation, empathy and ownership. Being committed to a common vision and having transparent communications."

Karen has succeeded globally by having the courage and the desire to step out of her comfort zone. For her, this means sometimes leaving your family and your own country.

"Ideation, empathy and execution" are some of the skills Karen has brought to the table, and these skills have given her an edge over others. Karen is good at focusing on new initiatives, and she is always able to find connections between seemingly disparate phenomena, and she makes things happen. No wonder Karen highlights that "Setting goals and getting things done" are the attitudes she has adopted throughout her life.

As Karen grows in her career, she would like to write more, writing, particularly about the insights not yet sighted. A global graduate, according to Karen, is someone who has networking experience, leadership abilities, and has a team spirit. And if she were hiring a recent graduate, these are the exact skills she will look for.

Her thoughts, insights and advice for recent graduates or any one about to step out into the world, is to "Learn new languages and understand other cultures. At the end of the day, personality is more important than your actual skills.

Finally, it is also important to demonstrate honesty and accountability."

Karen says if she had to do it all over again, maybe she would take more risks and work in as many countries as she could, as well as learn new languages and different cultures. Her next career move will be in line with following her instincts, but having a worst-case scenario in mind.

Jochem Bokhorst

With Jochem in Amsterdam

IF Google was a person, it would be Jochem, because he is one of my go-to people for the right kind of information on most things. Hanging out with Jochem is a journey of calm discovery: one minute you are learning something new on the Internet, and next he is telling you about photos he took of different birds or general wildlife in India, or plans that he is making to visit Portugal for his summer holidays. Jochem is currently exploring a new role as Content Manager for an online media company in The Netherlands.

Earlier, his work was mainly for the American market, but Jochem now works mainly for the Dutch market, acting as a mediator between the Client, freelance production people and partners, by making sure the work produced is of really good quality.

When it comes to a global feel at work, Jochem says, "There is never a shortage of an international flavour as there are people from Romania, Sweden and Mexico present in the same office, and there is always one language or another near the coffee machine."

Before getting his current job, he was planning on becoming a freelance Copywriter, so he started in-house copy writing for the same company. He took on more work, helping a friend out. It was not a regular "9 to 5 job", but he stayed until things were done, and he was always looking for ways to improve. Despite all his noble efforts, he unfortunately lost his job because the company was losing too much money and needed to cut down on the number of people employed and because he did not have a permanent contract, he was let go.

Jochem went on to freelance, but he kept in touch with his network. He had earlier covered for someone on holiday, ranging from two days to a week. His proactive attitude and his experience came in handy. Jochem had already proven himself useful in the past, because even without a contract, he had 200 website orders per week in high weeks and would constantly deliver on his task. Jochem was reconnected by a friend and was hired. This meant that Jochem started this role before he finished his Master's studies.

Jochem believes it is always worth investing in people, and in his own way, he tries to have a professional relationship with other freelancers. From first-hand experience, he knows how lonely it can be as a freelancer. He says of the experience, "One doesn't always have company or the benefit of a team or colleagues in the traditional working environment." Jochem likes to ask the various freelancers he works with, about their day and as well as have relevant small talk with them. From all these experiences, Jochem says he has learnt, "To always take note of the context a person is working in, and adapt to that. One has to be willing to put the other person first."

Jochem's journey to become a Content Manager hasn't always been a straight path. He started working in a part-time job in a nightclub picking up bottles and glasses.

I have observed that in my country Ghana and possibly in some African countries, students will shy away from a work experience like that and end up missing out on a variety of life experiences and transferable skills.

Whilst at University, Jochem wrote for his Faculty magazine, and was Chief Editor for a magazine on Geography: this magazine was by and for students on the Geography course. Jochem started as a photographer for the magazine, and also wrote articles for one year. He then acted as a Collaborating Editor, till his third year. Clearly, Jochem likes to seize opportunities and learn.

Jochem was brought up by parents with immense exposure, who played a lot of international music at home. This simple act fuelled his curiosity and influenced his opinion about the wider world. The playlist at home, he says, "Would cut across different music genres, like Peruvian, Chilean, Yiddish, Russian, classical, and church music."

Jochem's global outlook is therefore driven by his

curiosity about places, international studies and what happens outside his home country of The Netherlands.

Jochem says some of his teachers from primary school are not surprised he studied Human Geography, as he always found cultures interesting. Some of the key things which were a turning point for his curiosity, he recalls, was making projects about Surinam, a Dutch colony; and studying about aboriginals in his early days at school.

His Bachelor's degree took him to India twice. The first time he went to India was with fellow students for a course on marine resource management in Chennai, followed by his Bachelor's research. Most of the other people on the trip had already travelled outside of Europe on their own before, some even to India. He recalls, "For me, it was the first time outside of Europe."

At some points of the trip, Jochem felt he was comparing himself to his more experienced travelled friends. A taxi ride from the airport to the hotel was a real cultural shock. A big learning curve for him was when he arrived in India and saw rats on the streets and bats in the sky in Mumbai. The weather was humid, and traffic rules were non-existent.

Jochem quickly decided this was going to be the norm in his new environment, and he had to deal with it. Adopting this attitude helped him become more independent. Jochem says he was developing his own character along the way on these journeys, and it wasn't just a matter of research to fulfil an academic requirement.

Although Jochem already knew and spoke English, India changed a lot of things for him. He realised his English was good enough for constant interaction and this built his confidence to use the language for four months.

Jochem was also in Brazil to work on a sustainability project on reforestation for Symbeyond Research Group (now operating as Polre Advisory) - a company he co-founded with friends from University, to look at the sustainability of projects for private individuals, NGOs and companies. He was a researcher and vice chairman for the company for a year.

As someone who is very passionate about the environment, Jochem was in Ghana twice to conduct research for his thesis on: "The Impact of Forest Governance, Arrangements on the Livelihoods of Bushmeat Actors in Ghana's High Forest Zone" for his Master's degree.

Has Jochem missed any opportunities along the way? Jochem was refreshingly honest to say he was slow with finishing his studies. This affected everything else: graduation, and hunting for jobs in his field of study was delayed as a result.

All these he confesses was because he was a bit lost and not sure what to do at the time.

Jochem's most valuable skills are being extremely patient and detail-oriented, as well as being a good communicator. He believes that these skills are crucial for communicating to get the best information. Knowing what he knows now, in the future, Jochem would like to be more involved in training. Jochem got his wish, because in the summer of 2015, his company sent him to Australia, where he spent seven weeks to train and help the team there.

He encourages young graduates to evaluate things for

themselves. He found that some of the interns he worked with in Ghana do not think critically, or question things, or dig deep enough, but rather they believe things easily and accept things on face value. As a Ghanaian who trains a lot of young graduates, I can identify with these sentiments, and this is something I am working really hard to change. Jochem's advice to graduates is, "To be curious and think for yourself."

Jochem says, "In my eyes, a global graduate is someone with a global look on life, who doesn't think in boxes, but is open to the world around him or her; someone who looks at life with curious interest and a critical outlook."

Jochem was very kind to offer me his flat in Amsterdam as my hub, so I could travel across Europe to personally interview some of the equally amazing global graduates featured in this book.

Conclusions

WHEN I was 10 or 11 years old, my Dad would send me postcards with the pictures of the various colleges at Oxford University or the University of London. He encouraged me to study hard, so I would be able to go to one of those colleges or an Ivy league school in the USA, and then work for Goldman Sachs. My dad envisioned me as a top Finance Executive moving between cities in a matter of days, negotiating business deals. I guess this in a way, was my dad's idea of a Global Graduate.

I know my dad meant well, and although I haven't worked in Goldman Sachs, this book took me to Lithuania, Berlin, Amsterdam and Iceland in 48hours. I have gone on to start my own Global Graduate Academy, where I am training, coaching, mentoring and grooming the next generation of African graduates, entrepreneurs, business leaders, world leaders and change makers to be global superstars who will positively represent the continent. I have followed my own path, taken risks and gotten out of my comfort zone. I am my own kind of Global Graduate.

The individuals profiled in this book had their take on who a 'Global Graduate' is, and this goes to show, there is no single conclusive definition of the term. What we can all agree on, is that, among other things, you can excel anywhere if you're willing to: get out of your comfort zone, take risks (whether calculated or not), stay curious, prepare for opportunities, have a learning spirit, apply yourself and associate with the right people.

From the stories we've read, one cannot rule out how parents, guardians, mentors, friends, bosses, organisations like AIESEC and AFS and even situations and events in one way or the other can influence our career paths positively or negatively. In the case of this set of Global Graduates, it has been positive for the most part.

When one of my editors mentioned that she wished she had read a book like this growing up, because she would have aspired for more, I knew I was doing something right by putting together these stories. Even more profound, is the fact that she hopes to be a better parent by exposing her children to opportunities, and giving them the freedom to start exploring opportunities early. What a great attitude to have.

In Iceland, I was blessed to meet a very wise man, Kolbeinn Sigurðsson, who is a Biochemist as well as a Pastor, who has travelled extensively across Africa. And as someone who is always recruiting team members, Kolbeinn shared the story of two men, who were hired in the morning to get apples from the apple tree. They were supposed to take the apples to the market, sell them and make a profit.

The first man shakes the tree and gets his apples quickly, and then takes them to the market. He sells them quickly for 2000 ISK. The second man climbs the tree, plucks the apples, polishes the apples and sells them for 5000 ISK. The morale of the story is to do everything with excellence, and never let ambition take away the beauty.

For me, this sums up these sets of Global Graduates profiled. Their ambition and desire for excellence actually makes their real life stories beautiful and inspiring. Just don't be surprised to see this set of Global Graduates change paths and careers. Be surprised if it's not even more inspiring, because it will be.

I do, however, hope that their journeys will teach us a thing or two, and more importantly, we will be challenged to evaluate our own journeys and be inspired to make changes if we have to.

With Kolbeinn in Iceland

Acknowledgements

WITHOUT God, I am nothing. In him I am and hope to become!

I am eternally grateful to all the 35 Global Graduates featured in this book. Thank you for sharing your stories with me.

I am grateful to my parents Ms Rejoice Amekudzie and Mr Emmanuel Adjaho for the sacrifices they made in order for me to get a world-class education and exposure.

Thank you Uncle- Honourable Doe Adjaho for all the global opportunities you've given all of us who aspired for more.

Mr Eamonn Delaney, thank you for mentoring me and building my confidence. I am grateful you challenged me to be curious and to get out of my comfort zone.

Mr. Reginald Laryea, (Gaddy) thank you for setting up a global company that gave most young Ghanaians an idea of what it takes to be a global professional. I am so grateful for all the opportunities you have given me and many others. You directly impacted my career and that of three other people profiled in this book. There are so many others who are movers and shakers of industry because you not only employed them, but coached them to be achievers. God bless you greatly.

Dr. Vanessa Tetteh, thank you for setting me on this incredible career path and for giving me a glimpse of what a Global Graduate should be. To think that my encounter with you as an undergraduate will shape me to impact other people's lives, is extraordinary. I am so grateful and may God bless you greatly. I am equally gratefully you took the time to edit this book, your great suggestions and feedback have made all the difference.

Margaret Nettey, Beatrice Anowah Brew, Adelaide Addy, Emmanuel Kwesi Danso, Kusi Boakye and Princess, I am really grateful for all the time you spent being my extra pair of eyes and editing this work at various stages . This book came out better because of your feedback and input. I am equally gratefully to Selase, Misha, Laila, Petra, Sandister, Tillmann, Jochem, Lucien and Saulius, who also cross checked their stories and made amendments.

George Asamani, thank you for connecting me to Eva-Maria Olbers and also for recommending your colleagues Palvi and Nicole. Eva-Maria Olbers, thank you for introducing me to Louise and Catalina. Jochem, thank you for making me feel at home in Amsterdam at no extra cost. The Ghanaians I ran into in Antwerp (Alhaji, Bro Kofi and Irene Kyei Baffour (Sister Ama) when I missed my bus to Zurich. I came to you as a stranger and left a friend. You hosted me for days, so I can keep this dream alive. Thank you.

Samuel Polley, thank you for hosting me in Zurich. Anita Solomon, thank you for giving me a place to sleep in Zurich.

Ruth, thank you for introducing me to Bryndís Eva

Vilhjálmsdóttir. Bryndís thank you for introducing me to Kolbeinn. Kolbeinn, thank you for all the wisdom and insight.

Kweku, thank you for introducing me to Ruben Ahiakpote. Ruben, you did a brilliant cover for this book. Your creativity is amazing. Tillmann Schneider, thank you for hosting me in Berlin. Bastian Kojo Schneider, thank you for always hosting me in Berlin and for taking my profile photo for the book.

Anyone I met on the plane, in the train, on the bus, at waiting areas, who was curious to see in most cases the only black girl, and wondered what my story was. I am glad you asked, listened and encouraged me, thank you. I am equally grateful to everyone who made my stay pleasurable in all the countries I visited, particularly my new family and friends in Iceland. Listing your names will be another book. God bless you richly.

Prince, you really are a man's best friend. I know you can't read, but all those lonely and difficult times, when I locked myself up for days, hoping and searching for inspiration, you were the only familiar face that gave me a reason to hang on, laugh and keep writing. Thank you.

Augustine, Marcus, Henry, Kafui, Nana and the other students who volunteered to be trained in my garage for six weeks for the first Global Graduate Academy, you gave me hope for something big, including this book.

Sample Questionnaire for The Global Graduate Book

1. What do you currently do?

2. Did you always know what you wanted to do?
    2a. What did you study at University? (Undergraduate, Postgraduate /Master's/MBA, PhD, etc.)
    2b. Which university/universities did you attend?

3. What were some of the possible career paths you considered?

4. How did you get into your current role? Was it competitive?

5. What were your past roles (and where)?

6. What are some of the things you learnt from your past roles that have prepared you for this current one? (It could be the good, bad or ugly)

7. What do you recall to be your first ever global encounter?

8. Is there any one person, thing or situation that has influenced your thinking in a global direction?

9. Where are you from, and how many countries have you worked in? (please list them)

10. Which countries have you lived in, studied in or travelled to? Did you learn anything from this/these places?

11. Have you always had a global mindset? If yes, In what way?

12. Which global collaborations have you been involved in? (this can include conferences, meetings, concerts, etc. No limits, please)

13. What were some of the learning points from these collaborations? (Or what was the key learning point for you?)

14. What drives you to be global in your outlook?

15. Have you missed any opportunity/opportunities as a result of not being strategically global in your outlook? (This could be past or present)

16. What does it take to succeed globally, and how have you done it?

17. What edge do you have over others? And what skills / attitudes have you brought to the table?

18. What one skill / attitude do you think did it for you, or does it for you every time?

19. Which skill(s)/attitude(s) have you had to learn quickly?

20. Moving forward, which skill(s)/attitude(s) would you like to learn or demonstrate more of?

21. What have been some of the challenges of being in a global environment?

22. Who, to you, is a global graduate? If you were hiring a recent graduate, what would you look out for?

23. Your thoughts, insights and advice for Africans, Europeans, Asians and Americans? (Choose graduates from one group or continent and advise them. You are free to make it general for recent graduates or any one about to step out into the world)

24. If you had to do it all over again, would you do anything differently?

25 What is your greatest career highlight?
    25a. What is next for you?